Thomas Rettstatt

Provence

50 selected valley and mountain walks from the Ardèche to the
Verdon Gorge and from Mont Ventoux to the Calanques

With 76 colour photographs, 50 1:25.000 /1:50.000 / 1:150.000 walking
maps plus 2 overview maps with a scale of 1:1.000.000 / 1:2.500.000

ROTHER · MUNICH

Front cover:
The picturesque Moustiers-Ste-Marie at the foot of impressive crags.

Frontispiece (photo on page 2):
View into the Gorges de l'Ardèche from the Belvédère de la Madeleine.

All photographs by the author, with the exception of the photos on
pages 85, 136 right and 139 (Edwin Schmitt).

Cartography:
All maps © Bergverlag Rother GmbH

Translation:
Tony Pearson

The descriptions of all the walks given in this guide are made according
to the best knowledge of the author. The use of this guide is at one's
own risk. As far as is legally permitted, no responsibility will be
accepted for possible accidents, damage or injury of any kind.

1st edition 2000
© Bergverlag Rother GmbH, München

ISBN 3-7633-4801-8

Distributed in Great Britain by Cordee, 3a De Montfort Street, Leicester
Great Britain LE1 7HD, www.cordee.co.uk
in USA by AlpenBooks, 3616 South Road, C-1, Mukilteo,
WA 98275 USA, www.alpenbooks.com

ROTHER WALKING GUIDES

Crete West · Iceland · Mallorca · Mont Blanc · Norway South · Provence · Sardinia · Valais East ·
Around the Zugspitze

**Dear mountain lovers! We would be happy to hear your opinion and
suggestions for amendment to this Rother walking guide.**

BERGVERLAG ROTHER · Munich
D-85521 Ottobrunn · Haidgraben 3 · Tel. 0049/89/608669-0, Fax -69
Internet http://www.rother.de · E-mail bergverlag@rother.de

Preface

The Provence, the land of light and lavender. Who isn't familiar with it? Numerous tourists visit this holiday region in the south of France. Most seek out the sea or visit the splendid cultural monuments, but the number of walkers is also steadily increasing. Nevertheless, even in the high season, with the exception of such magnetic attractions as the Verdon Gorge, it is still possible to find unfrequented walks.

As the area is relatively large, an attempt has been made to find something for every taste: classics, which as a visitor to the Provence one simply has to see; solitary walks, which one can regard as secret tips; short, simple walks for children and elderly walkers; walks around towns for those interested in culture; long and difficult walks, as well as proper mountain routes. The gorges which are most worth visiting have also been included, and a short note has been made of the many places of interest, both cultural and landscape, as visits to these properly round off a trip to the Provence.

It is especially the contrasts which strike one in this unique landscape: mountains up to 2000 metres, deep gorges, caves, broad plains, the sea with its beaches and cliffs, beautiful forests, the Garrigue and desert-like expanses, as well as a rich flora and fauna. Nature conservation has also been gaining ground through the creation of new parks. Finally, particular note has to be made of the outstanding cuisine and the excellent wines.

In particular I would like to thank my wife, who accompanied me on my walks and who has supported me in the work on this guide, as well as Bergverlag Rother, who made this book possible. Thanks too are owed to Mme Busuttil in Mollans and Mme Hertzog in Violès for their help.

In this area as in others, factors such as forest fires and road building can bring about changes, so the publisher and the author would be grateful for any new information from walkers in the Provence.

Thomas Rettstatt

Contents

Steep cliffs and deep-blue sea – picture book landscape at Cassis.

8

Tourist Information

Use of the Guide

The most important information for each of the suggested walks is summarised as a list of key points. After a short description of the main characteristics of the walk, a detailed route description is given. As a rule the names are written as in the French IGN maps. All geographic places of importance are listed in the index at the end of the book. Finally there is a map, which gives an overview of the location of the individual walks.

Difficulty of Walks

Many of the walks follow marked routes and paths. Nevertheless, the markings, signposts and the characteristics of the paths are nothing like as exemplary as, for example, in the German-speaking Alpine areas. A sense of direction and a compass are therefore often necessary. Some walks also demand fitness, sure-footedness and a head for heights. Moreover, after periods of bad weather difficulties increase, and some routes even become impossible. So that the difficulties of the suggested routes can be better assessed, the route numbers are colour-coded as follows:

Blue These routes are generally well marked, reasonably wide and only moderately steep, so that they can be done with relatively little danger, even in poor weather. They can normally be safely undertaken by children and elderly people.

Red These routes are generally adequately marked, but often narrow and can be exposed over short sections. They should, therefore, only be attempted by sure-footed mountain walkers.

Black These paths are often adequately marked, but are frequently narrow and steep. In parts they can be exposed and sometimes use of the hands will be necessary (i.e. scrambling). These routes should, therefore, only be undertaken by sure-footed walkers with a head for heights, a good level of fitness and a good sense of direction.

Dangers

Most of the walks follow proper and generally well-marked paths; where walks are exposed or demanding this is pointed out in the text. It is only in spring in higher areas that snow can ever be a problem; fog would create navigation problems on some routes. Moreover, routes through gorges are sometimes not passable after heavy rainfall. A severe problem is that of forest fires – some regions can therefore be closed in high summer (especially Alpilles, Montagne Ste-Victoire).

Best Time of Year

Spring, early summer or autumn are the recommended times for lowland and coastal walks; for other areas early summer or autumn is recommended. On account of the great heat in the middle of summer, only the mountains in the High Provence, Mont Ventoux and the Montagne de Lure should be visited. In spring one must often reckon with large volumes of fast-flowing water in the streams and rivers.

Equipment

Stout shoes with a good tread, hard-wearing trousers, and a waterproof are required, and for mountain walks protection against wind and cold, a bivouac sack and bandages are needed, plus sufficient food and drink, as there is generally nowhere to obtain refreshment. For some walks a torch is necessary, and trekking poles and a pair of binoculars will provide good service.

Maps

Maps with the routes marked are provided for each of the suggested walks. They are a fundamental part of this guide. If you wish to purchase additional maps, then the excellent 1: 25.000 IGN walking maps, which cover the entire area, are recommended. The 1:50.000 Didier Richard maps which are based on the IGN maps are also good, but do not cover the whole region; at present the following sheets are available: 14, 19, 21, 24, 27, 28.

Walking times

Times given are for actual walking time with no time for stops. Such times are, however, always somewhat subjective. The total time is always given, and where possible, there are separate ascent and descent times, and in some cases times for the individual sections of the walk.

Bases

Huts as found in the Alps are practically non-existent, and other places to stop at en route are few and far between. The so-called Gîtes d'étape offer overnight accommodation with food and are to be found along the long-distance walking routes (GR Grande Randonnée), mostly in the proximity of valleys. Otherwise it is only in towns and villages that there is anywhere to stay or get food.

Approach

The public transport system is somewhat lacking, and outside the main towns the various starting points are only to be reached with difficulty, if at all, by public transport. Therefore, there is generally a short description of how to drive to the starting point.

The famous rock arch over the Ardèche at Vallon-Pont-d'Arc.

Conservation and environmental protection

The Provence offers many areas of natural beauty. Although there are still some shortcomings, conservation is on the increase, and is to be seen in the creation of new protected areas. As a walker ensure that you respect the environment, do not disturb any animals or pick any plants, keep to the paths, take your rubbish away with you, do not throw any cigarette ends away and avoid open fires, as there is often an acute risk of fire.

Walking in the Provence

Geography
The area of the Provence covered by this guide consists of the Départements Gard (only the eastern part), Vaucluse, Bouches-du-Rhône and Alpes-de-Haute-Provence. The Var and Ardèche Départements are only touched upon. Numerous mountain massifs, most of which are limestone, cut through the Provence: eastern foothills of the Cevennes (629m), Mont Ventoux (1910m), Dentelles de Montmirail (734m) Alpilles (387m), Luberon (1125m), Ste-Victoire (1011m), Ste-Baume (1147m), Étoile (778m) with Garlaban (710m), Montagnes de Lure (1825m) and the Pre Alps of the Haute Provence (1930m). The area is drained by three large rivers: the Rhone, the Durance and the Verdon) and many smaller ones (such as the Ardèche, Gard, Aigues, Ouvèze, Sorgue, Nesque, Calavon, Asse and Bléone). These have created the wonderful gorges – one of the main sights of the Provence – and the marsh landscape of the Camargue. The list of natural wonders is completed by the caves. Of course, there are hardly any lakes, just some artificial reservoirs. The largest and most important city is Marseille (pop. 1.2 million). Approximately 90% of the inhabitants live in the heavily-industrialised Rhone Valley areas and on the coast; the rest of the area is sparsely inhabited and predominantly agricultural.

Flora and Fauna
The flora is very rich. Amongst the most well-known plants are lavender, broom and the numerous herbs (rosemary, thyme, marjoram, basil, sage). Also there are lots of fruit and vegetables and a very good wine. Beautiful flowers include iris, tulips, hyacinth, heather, clover, primula, campanula, daphne, liverwort and yellow foxgloves. In areas where there have not been any forest fires, unique forests are to be found: up to 800m – holm and kermes oak, strawberry trees, mastic trees, juniper and pines; up to 1800m – chestnuts, maple, oak and beech; up to 2000m pine, fir, larch and spruce. One particularly special type of vegetation in the Provence is the Garrigue, generally a result of deforestation. It consists of low, often thorny shrubs, such as broom, thistle, juniper, rock roses, etc.
The fauna is also very varied. There are several poisonous snakes (asp viper, adder, Montpellier snake), rare birds of prey (such as Bonellis eagle, eagle owl, peregrine falcon, imperial eagle, Egyptian vulture) more than a hundred other bird species and numerous frogs, crab and fish species, and mammals such as beaver, marmot, deer wild boar and the badger.

The bright yellow of flowering broom in the Provencale spring.

Friendly donkeys on a meadow at la Palud-sur-Verdon.

National parks
Luberon Nature Reserve (Parc naturel régional): In 1977 almost the complete mountain area and part of the Vaucluse Plateau came under protection (many rare animals and plants). The park includes about 140,000 hectares. Ensure that you follow the regulations in order to preserve the natural beauty of the area.

Camargue Nature Reserve (Parc naturel régional). In 1970 almost the complete estuary area between the greater and lesser Rhone consisting of 85,000 hectares became protected. The aim of the park is to protect nature, especially the bird world and the Camargue horses and cattle and to enable the population to maintain their traditional way of life in harmony with nature. As far back as 1927 the Étang de Vacarrès became a national reserve under particularly strong protection: it cannot be entered.

Haute Provence Geological Nature Reserve (Réserve naturelle géologique): In 1984 a protected zone of 149,000 hectares was created, which included a nature reserve of 269 hectares in 18 different places in the Département Alpes-de-Haute-Provence. Its purpose was to protect the rich deposits of fossils. In the protected zone there are only slight restrictions on fossil gathering, but in the core areas every type of fossil gathering activity is prohibited.

Long-distance walks (Grandes Randonnées = GR)
Numerous long distance walking paths (such as GR 6 and 9) lead through the Provence. The descriptions for these are mainly in French. At the end of each section of a GR there is a Gîte d'étape: a simple hostel where one can spend the night and eat.

Information and Addresses

Camping
Informal camping is generally forbidden. One of the many official campsites should therefore be used.

Climate
The climate in the Provence is characterised by its mildness and the amount of sunshine. The total amount of precipitation is greater than one might at first expect: in early spring and autumn there are heavy showers, and thunderstorms are to be reckoned with from May to October. In the height of summer it is dry and except in the High Provence, it is hot (often above 30° C). Spring, with its fruit harvest, is very changeable. In early summer many different plants are in flower and the weather becomes more stable. There is a lot of sunshine from July to the middle of September, after which it becomes more changeable. The mistral, a strong, dry fall wind from the north, can be very treacherous, causing temperatures to drop by up to 10° C. Strong winds can be encountered on Mont Ventoux and the Montagne de Lure.

Emergency phone numbers
Police/breakdown: 17; Fire brigade/Ambulance: 18

The Roman triumphal arch »Arc municipal« in St-Remy de Provence.

A walk into the past – the ruins of Glanum.

Getting there

For driving to the Provence there is a good network of motorways through France by which one can approach the Rhone Valley. The motorway along the Mediterranean also provides an approach from the direction of Italy.

All of the larger cities can be reached by train.

There are airports in Marseille-Marignane, Avignon, Nîmes and Nice.

Information

The following places in the Provence provide information:

■ *Gard:* Comité départemental du Tourisme: 3, place des Arènes, B.P. 122, 30011 Nîmes Cedex.

■ *Bouche-du-Rhône:* Comité départemental du Tourisme: 13, rue Roux de Brignoles, 13006 Marseille.

■ *Vaucluse:* Comité départemental du Tourisme: Quartier la Balance-Place Campana, B.P. 147, 84008 Avignon Cedex.

■ *Alpes-de-Haute-Provence:* Comité départemental du Tourisme: 19, rue du Dr. Honnorat, B.P. 170, 04005 Digne-les-Bains Cedex.

■ *Var:* Comité départemental du Tourisme: 1, Boulevard Foch, B.P. 99, 83003 Draguignan Cedex.

Mountain rescue

In case of emergency it is best to contact the Gendarmerie (emergency number 17), as they have a special unit for mountain rescue.

Public holidays and holiday periods
1 January, Easter Monday, 1 May, 8 May, the Ascension, Whit Monday, 14 July (National Holiday) 15 August, 1 November, 11 November, 25 December. The main holiday time is from the end of June to the end of August.

Snakes
There are several types of poisonous snakes in the Provence – adder, asp viper and Montpellier snake. It is therefore necessary to take care.

Sport
There are many opportunities for sport: riding, cycling (a popular sport), mountain biking (not so well known), canoeing and canyoning (especially in the big gorges), climbing (in the Hautes Provence) angling, etc.

Telephone
Dialling code for France: 0033

Theft
Cars are frequently broken into, especially in the larger towns or areas with lots of tourists, such as the Camargue, the Calanques or the Verdon Gorge. Never leave items of value in your car.

Transport
There are very good train connections on the main lines Orange-Avignon or Nîmes, and on the local lines Avignon-Cavaillon-Salon-Marseille and Siste-ron- Aix-Marseille there are 4 to 8 trains per day. Outside of the cities public transport is poor: (2-4 buses, often only on workdays), such as on the following important stretches: Avignon/Orange-Vaison, Carpentras-Malau-cène-Vaison, Avignon-Apt-Digne, Avignon-Fontaine-de-Vaucluse, Avignon-Lourmarin, Marseille-Aix-Lourmarin-Apt, Marseille-Aix-Riez. Taxis are to be found in all the larger places; car hire, however, generally only in the cities.

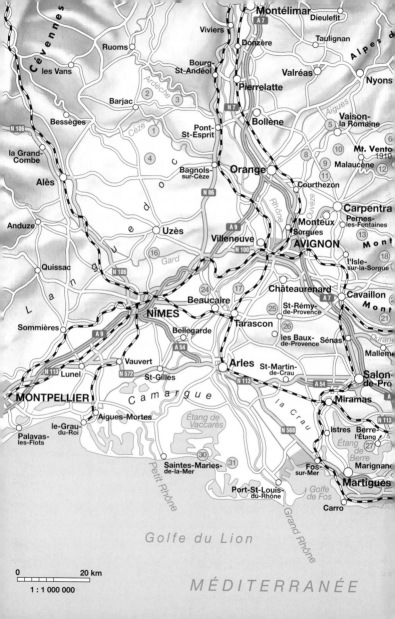

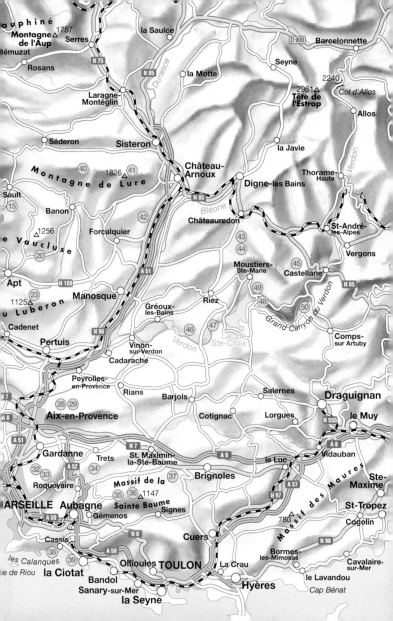

1 Gorges de la Cèze

Harsh garrigue landscape and an almost charming gorge

Mas Crémat – Gorges de la Cèze – le Clap – Mas Crémat

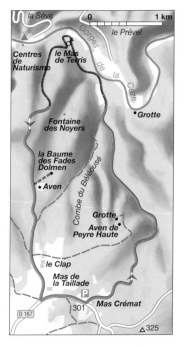

Location: St-Martin-d'Ardèche, 60m.

Starting point: Leave St-Martin via the D 141 and the D 901 in the direction of Barjac to drive through the Cèze Gorge on the D 980 after about 15km. At the end of the gorge take the minor D 167 on the right and park about 23km from St-Martin at Mas Crémat (301m) on the side of the forest road (L 9) which branches off.

Walking time: Mas Crémat – split rocks: 1¼ hrs; split rocks – Mas Crémat: 2 hrs; total time: 3¼ hrs.

Ascent: About 210m.

Lowest point: About 90m in the Gorges de la Cèze.

Grade: Easy walking on good forest tracks and some tarmac road. No problems regarding navigation.

Alternative: About 1km before le Clap it is possible to take a detour along a marked path (yellow waymarkings) to the Dolmen of Baume des Fades, which ought to be of interest, and not only to fans of Asterix and Obelix (about 15 min).

Places of Interest: A few kilometres downstream at la Roque is the most beautiful waterfall in the Provence, the Cascade du Sautadet (best time in Spring).

The wild, Mediterranean forest vegetation on the approach and return paths and the picturesque banks of the gorge with the peaceful Cèze mark the walk through this isolated area.

From the parking area at the **Mas Crémat** farmhouse take the forest road DFCI L 9 (signpost »La Cèze«) to the north. The wide road, which is rather stony in parts, leads gently downwards through an open Mediterranean forest of evergreen oak, sycamore and juniper trees. There is plenty of time here to enjoy the rich flora before the valley bottom is reached. Now after some distance the river is reached at the so-called **split rocks,** which the road cuts through (1¼ hrs). You can now continue along the forest road to the picnic place at the river, but it is better to go right immediately after the rocks and take the path which leads to the Cèze. Between the poplars and the river, the picturesque picnic area is reached at the base of the gorge (10 min). There are steep cliffs on the opposite riverbank. Now go back a few metres to the south to the track and follow the forest road marked with DFCI L 7, which leads back out of the gorge. This is somewhat narrower and stonier, and at the beginning somewhat steeper, than the road leading to the gorge. Go past the ruins of Terris and again cross through a beautiful Mediterranean forest. On a plateau the gravel road becomes almost level and after about 1½ hrs, at the farm called **le Clap,** it becomes a tarmaced road. The landscape changes too at this point, with low bushes becoming predominant. After about 500m, at the farmhouse Mas de la Taillade, the road meets the D 167. Follow this little-used road to the left back to the starting point (20 min).

The peaceful, tranquil landscape in the Gorges de la Cèze.

2 Bois de Ronze and Aven d'Orgnac

Through the typical Garrigue landscape of the Ardèche

Aven d'Orgnac – Plaine de Ronze Ouest – la Forestière – Aven d'Orgnac

Location: St-Martin-d'Ardèche, 60m.

Starting point: In St-Martin cross the river over a suspension bridge (D 141) and then go onto the well constructed D 901 as far as Laval; there go right on narrow, winding roads (D 174, D 217, D 317) as far as the car park at the Caves of Orgnac (300m), 17km from St-Martin-d'Ardèche.

Walking time: Aven d'Orgnac – D 217: a good 45 min; D 217 – P.385m – D 217: 1¼ hrs; D 217 – Aven d'Orgnac: just under 45 min; total time 2¾ hrs.

Ascent: About 100m.

Highest point: 385m on the Plaine de Ronze Ouest.

Grade: Easy walking on wide paths with little ascent. Some care is needed with directions, as not all of the paths are adequately marked.

Alternative: If you wish you can walk along the minor access road to Aven de la Forestière (about 45 min there and back).

Places of Interest: You should not miss visiting the Aven d'Orgnac, one of the most well-known and finest caves in the Ardèche. Warm clothing is recommended as the inside temperature is only 13° C. The Aven de la Forestière, with its slender stalactites and stalagmites, is hardly less spectacular.

This walk gives one an insight into the typical, evergreen garrigue landscape of the southern Ardèche at the foot of the Cevennes, whose dry, porous limestone ground has encouraged the formation of many splendid caves.

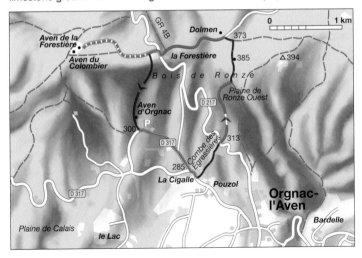

From the car park at **Aven d'Orgnac** walk a short distance to the south to the D 317, which is followed to the left. Go along the road without any notable change in height through a hilly, karst landscape to the lowest point on the route. About 200m past the second junction (285m) directly after the Centre d'accueil »La Cigale«, turn left onto a tarmaced road with yellow waymarkings, which leads with a scarcely perceptible rise, to the edge of Combe des Egressières, a dry valley with open scrub, and on to a holiday village on the D 217 (a good 45 min). Cross straight over the asphalted road. The path, which has faint blue waymarkings, goes gently uphill through a hilly garigue landscape in the direction of **Bois de Ronze**. After almost a kilometre the path curves to the right and shortly after meets a path coming from the south. This is followed to the left in a northerly direction. After a few hundred metres a junction with a noticeable oak tree marks the highest point of the walk (385m). The

Splendid stalactite formations in the caves of Aven d'Orgnac.

branch to the right is ignored and the path is followed onwards to the north as far as a junction of paths where the GR 4 B is met (45 min). Turn left here passing an overgrown dolmen and stay on the well-marked track. It leads directly through the garrigue landscape and offers repeated views of the surrounding hills. After 30 minutes the D 217 is crossed diagonally to the right (the new GR 4 B forks off to the right immediately before this), and this minor road is followed for a short distance to Aven de la Forestière. Soon, at the sign »Aven de la Forestière« the old faintly red and white waymarked GR 4 B turns off to the left (also yellow-white waymarkings). Go along this almost imperceptibly downhill through open scrub back to the car park at the Orgnac caves (almost 45 min).

3 Lower Ardèche Gorge

Rock faces of more than 100m in height line the calm, deep-green water

Sauze – St-Marcel – La Fève and back

Steep slopes in the Gorges de l'Ardèche.

Location: St-Martin-d'Ardèche, 60m.
Starting point: From St-Martin drive up-valley for about 2km on the D 290 and then turn left onto a small tarmac road which leads to the Sauze Camp Site (45m). Down to the right, next to the river, there is a large car park, at which one has to pay in summer.
Walking time: Sauze – St-Marcel: 1¼ hrs; St-Marcel – La Fève: 1½ hrs; La Fève – Sauze: 2¾ hrs; total time: 5½ hrs.
Ascent: Insignificant.
Highest point: 50m.
Grade: Long walk on mainly well-marked

paths. Sure-footedness and a bit of a head for heights are necessary on the sometimes narrow path. Increased care is needed if it is wet, as the path goes over worn and slippery rocks.
Alternative: It is also possible to extend the walk in the gorge as much as one likes: 1½ hrs after La Fève one reaches the wildest part, the Cirque de la Madeleine at Les Templiers, (n.b. A ford has to be crossed). An ascent out of the gorge is first possible after the Gournier Bivouac (1¾ hrs from Les Templiers; a further ford) from where a steep ascent leads back to the D 290 (good ¾ hr; return using a 2nd car or order a taxi).
Advice: The walk should not be undertaken in heavy rain, as the rocks are slippery and the river can rise. The best time of year is June to October: earlier than this the fords are generally impassable and there is too much water in the river. For information about the water level: tel: 0475386300.
Places of interest: One should not miss out on driving along the 35km long panoramic road situated high above the gorge. The many viewpoints (»Belvédères«) offer continual breath-taking views into the depths of the mighty gorge. The caves too on this side of the river are also worth a visit: the Grotte de St-Marcel, with its unique calcareous sinter terraces, over which the water flows; the Grotte de la Madeleine, with its many unusual colours and its stalactite formations; and the Aven de Marzal, the largest and most splendid of the caves.

After the Verdon Gorge the Ardèche Gorge is the most impressive gorge in the Provence. At first gentle, soon the rock faces rise up steeply and are mirrored in the green waters of the wide, placidly-flowing river.

The path along the river, which is marked with yellow or yellow-green waymarkings, (sometimes a bit faint) begins immediately to the north behind the **Sauze** campsite. Take heed of the notice at the beginning! The path leads repeatedly through green thickets, then the valley narrows, the sides become steeper and higher and one descends into the enchanting wilderness of the gorge. The rocky bank forces one at several points to make short ascents and descents, which can be tiring in the summer heat. On the rocks of the Ranc-Pointu viewpoint the first band of rocks above the river has to be overcome, whereby the worn steps demand sure-footedness and caution. After this the river makes a big curve to the west. Below the **Grotte de St-Marcel** the rocky terrain on the riverbank once again demands caution from the walker. On the opposite side of the river the rock overhangs of Castelviel and a skull-shaped individual cliff are passed. The recommended path continues in a north-westerly direction along the river. Evergreen chestnut oaks contrast with the bare, towering rock walls, which are reflected in the water. After a further 1½ hrs, opposite the rock wall of Remparts du Garn on a path which presents no further problems, the ford of **La Fève** is reached – the point from where the walk returns.

The same path leads in 2¾ hrs back to the car, allowing a completely different perspective.

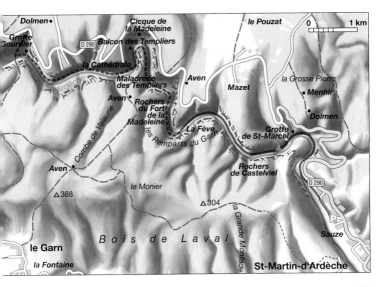

4 Les Concluses

A bizarre gorge with overhanging rock walls and potholes

Combe St-Martin – Grotte des Boeufs – le Portail – Combe St-Martin

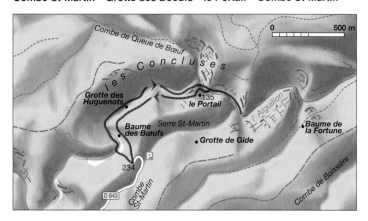

Location: Uzès, 138m.

Starting point: In Uzès take the wide D 979 to the north to Lussan. From here first go along the narrow D 143, then the D 643 to the car park at Concluses (234m), 24km from Uzès.

Walking time: 40 min to Portail; excursion to the gorge and back to Portail: About 25 min; Return to car park: 25 min; total time: 1½ hrs.

Ascent: About 100m.

Lowest point: Le Portail, 135m.

Grade: The walk to Portail requires some sense of direction and sure-footedness, particularly on the highly-polished rocks in the bed of the stream. The direct, yellow waymarked normal route to Portail (the return path for this walk) is easy and

accessible to everybody. It also offers beautiful impressions of the Concluses. (45 min there and back).

Advice: The walk along the stream bed is only possible in summer when the river has largely dried up (not before the beginning of June) and water is only present in some deep holes. Otherwise the normal route can be taken.

Places of Interest: The viewpoint of Guidon du Bouquet west of Lussan offers a broad panoramic view of Mont Ventoux, the Cevennes and Alpilles. In Uzès the picturesque old town with the Place aux Herbes, the castle (Duché) with interior decoration and the Campanile of the cathedral all provide an interesting alternative to walking.

The Concluses is the most interesting part of a gorge which the Aiguillon has cut deep into the limestone cliffs. Overhanging cliffs, enormous potholes and deep pools in the riverbed give this cool, gloomy place its curious charm.

From the **car park** do not take the direct marked path to Portail (to the right) but rather the unmarked path to the left, which goes downhill very steeply. The gorge is reached through the rampant, evergreen garrigue vegetation. On the way there are repeated impressive views of the cliffs opposite. On reaching the dried-up riverbed, follow this to the east (right) more or less without a path. At the **Grotte des Bœufs** keep to the path cut out along the Aiguillon, surrounded by bizarre rock walls until **Portail** is reached (40 min). This is a sort of gateway, for the rocks close above the walker leaving only a small gap. From here one should, depending on the height of the water and one's mood, carry on for a couple hundred metres along the streambed into the most beautiful part of the gorge, (i.e. until it opens again somewhat, nearly 15 min, easy). The walls rise up steeply, deep green pools and potholes line the way. Sometimes it is necessary to take off one's shoes.

Back at Portail, take the path to the left (yellow way marks), which is rocky, but provides a mainly gentle ascent out of the gorge. The **car park** is reached again after about 25 min.

Shade and peace in the Concluses at Portail – the narrowest point.

27

5 Vaison-la-Romaine

A mediaeval town with many Roman remains

Church – Quartier de Puymin – Upper town – Church

Location: Vaison-la-Romaine, 193m.
Starting point: Car park by the former cathedral of Notre-Dame-de-Nazareth.
Walking time: Pure walking time over a good 3km about 1 hr (without a walk through the excavations); with visits one should allow half a day.
Ascent: Negligible.
Highest point: Castle (about 250m).
Refreshment: Bars and cafes in town.
Alternative: In addition one can make an excursion into the beautifully-situated mediaeval town of Crestet – a varied route through woods and vineyards. From Vaison go left at the Roman bridge (D 938) and immediately to the right onto a yellow waymarked path as far as the castle road. Here go left and after 50 metres right, then left again along the yellow-red waymarked path to Crestet (walking time about 1¾ hrs).

The small, picturesque town on the Ouvèze offers, in addition to its many well-preserved Roman monuments and a romantic mediaeval upper town, the opportunity for a leisurely town walk.

From the **car park** one should begin by visiting the adjacent cathedral of N.-D.-de-Nazareth. The Romanesque building from the 10th to 12th century was erected on the remains of Roman buildings (worth-seeing: Romanesque main altar, 12th century cloister with remains of early Christian art).

From the church take the wide Av. Jules Ferry to the east and at the end turn left into the Av. Général de Gaulle. 100m further on at the upper end of the Place du 11-Novembre the Roman excavations of the **Quartier de la Villasse** are to be found on the left. Go past the remains of the baths and the basilica (both on the left) to the so-called »House of the Silver Busts« (right). The enormous house with many rooms, courts and gardens indicates the luxury enjoyed by a rich family. The same is true of the »House of the

Dauphin« to the west of it. After the circular walk go diagonally left over the road to Place Sautel with its entrance to the second Roman excavations, the **Quartier de Puymin**. Here is the »House of Messier«, a good insight into the splendid life of an aristocratic family. This is followed by the columned courtyard of Pompeius, which is surrounded by an ornamental garden. Past a block of flats and a pump room one comes to the museum, which has some interesting finds (including statues of Hadrian and his wife, Sabina, a ruler in armour, the silver busts which were found in the »House of the Silver Busts« and a number of mosaics). Go past the block of flats to finally reach the Roman theatre to the north, comparable with the one in Orange, but somewhat smaller and less well preserved. From the Place Sautel go back to the south to the Av. Général de Gaulle and then left over the Cours Fabre to the shady Place Montfort with old plane trees, shops,

The quiet cloister in the Cathedral of Notre-Dame in Vaison-la-Romaine.

bars and restaurants. From there go right along the main road, the Rue de la République and then left into the pedestrian area (Grande Rue), the main shopping street. Go over the 2000 year-old Roman bridge with a 17m span to the left bank of the Ouvèze, cross the D 938 and go uphill along the Rue G. Gevaudan. At the Place du Poids turn left into the mediaeval **Upper Town**. Go up the narrow, cobbled Rue de l'Horloge with its old, mainly restored stone houses. From the 15th century church go straight on up a steep somewhat tiring path to the ruins of the castle with a fine view over the town and of Mont Ventoux. Back again to the church and then go left along the Rue des Fours to the picturesque Market Place and then right along the Rue de l'Évêché, both lined by old houses. Now go left along the Rue de l'Horloge and the Rue Gevaudan down to the river, which is crossed straight on along the Av. Cassin, which leads directly to the **car park**.

6   In the lower Gorges du Toulourenc

An unusual gorge trip including cave exploration

Pont de Veaux – Gorges du Toulourenc – Pont Vieux and back

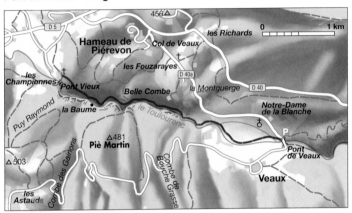

Location: Vaison-la-Romaine, 193m, in Ouvèze Valley.

Starting point: Leave Vaison on the D 938 through the Ouvèze Valley and then turn left twice, first onto the D 54 and then the D 13, which later becomes the D 5 (change of Département). Shortly before Mollans, take the D 40 on the right as far as the houses of Pas de Ventoux and then continue right on the narrow D 40 A as far as the Pont de Veaux (315m, small car park and further parking on the side of the road), about 16km from Vaison.

Walking time: Pont de Veaux – Gorges du Toulourenc – Pont Vieux: 2 hrs; return along the same route: 2 hrs; total time: 4 hrs. (This time is only an approximation with no allowance for changing shoes or clothes; it is very much dependent on the amount of water in the river).

Ascent: Negligible.

Lowest point: 300m at the Pont Vieux.

Grade: Although not marked, finding the way is not a problem. Sure-footedness on the slippery pebbles is necessary, as is being able to swim.

Advice: Solid shoes for swimming, a swimming costume and a waterproof plastic sack for the rucksack are absolutely necessary. A torch is also required for visiting the cave. The walk can only be undertaken with low water, i.e. in the period from mid June to the end of September. The gorge is to be avoided after heavy rain or thunderstorms; if in doubt contact the local authorities.

Places of Interest: A cave with wall paintings in the gorge.

This unusual walk offers much variety: a rugged gorge, which forces one to swim at some points, as well as a cave with a painting. The best months for the trip are in July and August when there is little water in the river and the cool wetness is pleasantly refreshing. It can, however, be rather cool in the morning as it is still in the shade.

From **Pont de Veaux** turn downstream towards the right bank of the river Toulourenc and follow a path which leads across the Veaux plateau towards the river after some distance through fields and garrigue vegetation. After a left-hand bend the river is reached again and beyond a farm the bed of the river, which is followed for the rest of the walk, is also reached. The Veaux plateau is now left behind and the wild gorge is entered. The scenery changes continually on this journey of discovery: deep pools with clear water, small rapids, steep cliffs, dark and narrow and then wider, delightful sections. The route continues along the side of the river over

The exciting route through the Gorges du Toulourenc with river crossings and cave exploration.

pebble banks, wading through the water or sometimes swimming as far as the **Pont Vieux** (about 2 hrs). Some sections can be avoided when the water is high by carefully following poor paths on the bank, sometimes one can only turn back. About half way along one should watch the right bank to avoid missing the cave entrance, which is at a narrow section with a steep wall. On the left wall of the cave there is, according to the discoverer, Paul Belin, the drawing of an African elephant from 200 BC (Hannibal's crossing of the Alps). This is however, scarcely decipherable for a layman. Either one needs the book by Paul Belin – »La Grotte de l'éléphant d'Hannibal« (out of print) or a knowledgeable guide. Information can be obtained from Mme S.Buix from the organisation »Patrimoine, Histoire et Culture des Baronnies«, La Roncelière, Le Grand Chemin, F-26170 Buis-les-Baronnies. Otherwise, it is still fun to explore by oneself. Do not, however, add to the modern scribblings.

7 Mont Ventoux, 1910m

A wild wind-formed mountain landscape with an Alpine character

Mont Serein – Mont Ventoux – Tête de la Grave – Mont Serein

Location: Vaison-la-Romaine, 193m, in the Ouvèze Valley.

Starting point: From Vaison drive along the wide D 938 to Malaucène and then turn left along the well-constructed panoramic road, the D 974 to Mont Ventoux. About 15km from Malaucène go right onto the D 164A to the winter sports town of Mont Serein (1400m), where the road ends at a campsite with plenty of parking, 26km from Vaison.

Walking time: Mont Serein – Mont Ventoux: 1¾ hrs; Mont Ventoux – Tête de la Grave: 1½ hrs; Tête de la Grave – Mont Serein: nearly 2¼ hrs; total time: nearly 5½ hrs.

Ascent: About 510m.

Grade: Mountain walk with alpine character on well-marked paths, which requires sure-footedness and a head for heights especially on the scree slopes.

Alternative: If you only want to tick off the summit, you can return via the ascent route: 1¼ hrs.

Advice: In foggy conditions or strong winds (and it can get very windy here!) you are strongly recommended not to do this walk.

Places of Interest: Malaucène and Crestet: two typical Vaucluse towns with old centres. A drive along the ridge of Mont Ventoux is very worthwhile.

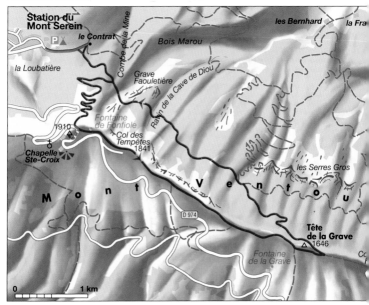

The summit of Mont Ventoux with the bare slopes of the south flank.

The ascent of Mont Ventoux is one of the finest mountain routes in the Provence. There is a fantastic panorama from its summit, and in clear weather the Alps, Cevennes and the Mediterranean can be seen.

From the **car park** go straight on along the closed tarmac road, and after a few minutes take a gravelled forest track with red and white GR markings on the right. The track, which is mainly level, continues through open pine forest to soon reach a fork (1430m). Take the right hand path marked red and white and ascend in long drawn out zigzags up the mountain. As height is gained the woods thin out, the vegetation becomes sparser, until there is only scree. This is compensated for by ever-improving views of the valley. The path touches the D 974 at a tangent (1750m) and winds on up the mountain over scree. At about 1800m there is a short spur path in a bend, which leads to the Fontaine de Fonfiole (spring), which is in a steep scree slope. Below the summit the road is reached; after a few minutes an orientation table with good views is passed and after a right-hand bend, the narrow road (right) is taken to **the summit**. A short ascent leads to the highest point in the Provence (1910m; 1¾ hrs), which is occupied by technical equipment and buildings. Go back along the wide D 974, first to the left then right, and then along a rocky path, (from here on marked as GR 4) which leads down between blue and red marking poles. This briefly touches the road again, then the path turns off to the left and the marker poles are followed along a

Scree slopes and crags on the wooded north side of Mont Ventoux.

tarmac road that ends at a military establishment. Go past this, first taking a stony path, which runs along the south side of the ridge. (Take care, as the ground drops away without warning on the north side and the rock is very friable). In the bare landscape it is possible to see remains of Arctic vegetation, such as a relation of the yellow alpine poppy; further on there are grasses again and low bushes at the side of the path. Steadily, and with continual good views, the path leads on downhill. Shortly after the hilltop of the **Tête de la Grave**, leave the red and white marked GR 4 (1640m; 1½ hrs) and turn off left at a cairn. The path, which now has yellow waymarkings, leads from the scree covered south side to the more heavily-wooded north side where it descends more steeply to the GR 9 (about 1400m; 40 min). At the junction follow the red and white markings to the left, ignoring a path which shortly after goes off right into the valley. The path to follow, the Serres-Gros High Route, named after a precipice below it to the right, proceeds gently up and down, mainly through forest. At several points it is necessary to cross steep scree gulleys, which offer dizzying views into the depths. The last two, the Cave de Diou and Grave Faouletière are the wildest and largest. Be careful on both of these traverses, especially if there is any remaining snow or if it is wet (great danger of slipping!), for the rock is very loose and there is a steep drop. Shortly after the last scree slope the approach path is reached which leads back to the starting point (1½ hrs).

The Serres-Gros High Route on the border between trees and crags.

8 Through the vineyards of Violès

Round-trip with views through a typical cultivated Provence landscape

Violès – D 977 – Plan de Dieu – la Bouveau – Violès

Location: Vaison-la-Romaine, 193m, in the Ouvèze Valley.

Starting point: From Vaison drive on the D 977 downstream towards Violès (96m), where it is possible to park at the stadium near the Ouvèze, 17km from Vaison.

Walking time: Violès – D 977: good 30 min; D 977 – D 67: just under 1 hr; D 67 – D 23 – first crossing: 30 min; D 23 – la Bouveau: 1 hr; la Bouvea – Violès: 1½ hrs; total time: 4½ hrs.

Ascent: About 60m.

Highest point: 133m on the high bank of the Ouvèze.

Grade: Almost level, yellow waymarked tracks or roads (some asphalted), which are undemanding: not, however, recommended when hot.

Alternative: The walk can be shortened if you return directly to Violès via the D 67 (45 min) or the small parish road at the Plan de Dieu (45 min).

Places of Interest: It is worth visiting Orange on account of its well-preserved Roman monuments (Theatre, Triumphal arch and Stadium) and its small old town.

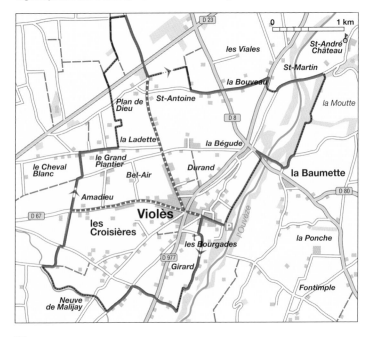

The branch in the Ouvèze at la Baumette.

This round-trip walk allows us to enjoy both the cultivated landscape of fields and vineyards created by man, as well as undisturbed natural landscapes, with small woods, the unspoilt bank of the Ouvèze (botanical nature trail) and the mountain chain in the background.

From the **car park,** go along the approach road (Rue du Stade, Place Général de Gaulle, Rue de la République) back to the Rue du Moulin, which goes left to the cemetery. From here follow yellow waymarkings left past the cemetery and on along the Chemin des Paluds. In front of the Girard farmhouse (right) go straight along the irrigation canal on the edge of the woods above the Ouvèze for about 300m. After crossing the canal take the Chemin du Gué on the right, passing the farm of the same name to arrive at the tarmaced road, the **D 977** (a good 30 min). Here, go straight on along the Chemin des Cyprès, which turns into the Chemin de Malijay after a little less than 300m, and which leads to the Canal de Carpentras. Now turn off right and follow the footpath along the irrigation canal. On the way a minor road is crossed at Neuve de Malijay with a view of the surrounding fields as far as the Dentelles de Montmirail. After a good 1km along the canal, turn right along a second tarmac road over a bridge and after a bend to the left arrive at a junction. Here go right and shortly after left again (Chemin des Rouvières) to reach the D 67 (just under an hr), which is crossed. The road ahead goes straight on apart from a right-left bend, until another junction (Chemin du

Vines at the Plan de Dieu with a view of the Dentelles de Montmirail.

Cheval blanc). Follow this to the right and after about 700m turn to the left along the yellow-marked vineyard trail in the direction of Violès. Go along this whereby the D 23 is crossed for the first time (30 min) and finally reach a small shady wood with truffle oaks. At the end of this take the first path on the left over the level stony plateau of **Plan de Dieu** with its vines until the circular route of Travaillan is reached (notice board). Here turn off right and at the end of the path go through the vines again to reach a tarmac road. Go along this, crossing the D 23 (30 min) a second time and a good 100m further on follow the stony path (marked yellow) through the vineyards as far as a couple of cherry trees. Here the waymarkings lead to the right following a path over a field to the asphalted Chemin St-Antoine. This leads left to the D 8. Cross this and after about 250m reach the **la Bouveau** farmhouse on the minor road of the same name (30 min). Continue to the D 977, turning right here and after about 100m taking a track on the left which shortly afterwards reaches a tarmaced road, where you go left again. This runs along the route of what

was once a railway line. Cross the Ouvèze over a viaduct and after 300m follow the markings to the right, where a botanical nature trail has been set up. The path skirts a well and after this take a path which goes up to the left over steps. At the end of this go to the right, passing cliffs and then make your way down a small valley, the stream in which is crossed via a footbridge. Further steps lead to the main bank again from where there are splendid views of the Dentelles de Montmirail, the Ouvèze Valley and the Violès plain. After the highest point of the walk the botanical trail leads back down into the valley. Go to the right past a rubbish tip onto the old Baumette bridge (a good hr) over the Ouvèze to the D 8, which is followed on the other side of the road to the left for a distance. The yellow waymarkings then go to the right and lead along the bank of the Ouvèze through a small wood back to the stadium in **Violès** (nearly 30 min).

9 Dentelles de Montmirail

Steep white rock pinnacles tower into the blue sky above green slopes

Les Florets – Col du Cayron – Rocher du Midi – Rocher du Turc – P. 277m – les Florets

Location: Carpentras, 102m.

Starting point: From Carpentras take the wide D 7 in a northerly direction. Stay on the D 7 after Vacqueyras (turn right) as far as Gigondas, where you follow the narrow minor road to the right to les Florets (350m, CAF hut, hotel and restaurant). The tarmac surface ends here at a spacious car park (a steep concreted section of road follows), 17km from Carpentras.

Walking time: Les Florets – Col du Cayron: 10 min; Col du Cayron – Rocher du Midi: 20 min; Rocher du Midi – Turning off for alternative route: 50 min; Turning off – P. 277m: 40 min; P. 277m – les Florets: 30 min; total time: 2½ hrs.

Ascent: About 370m.

Highest point: About 600m at Rocher du Turc (627m).

Grade: Half of the walk is gentle forest tracks, otherwise narrow, generally adequately-marked paths, which require sure-footedness.

Alternative: If you are not put off by a poor gravelled track, it is possible to drive to the Col du Cayron, which shortens the walk by 15 min. From the turning off after the Rocher du Turc it is possible to descend directly to the Col du Cayron via a wide but steep path. This marked path, which leads through shrubs, reduces the walking time by 50 min.

Advice: Gigondas is famous for its heavy red wine, Beaumes-de-Venise for its sweet white wine (Muscat).

Places of Interest: Carpentras is worth a visit on account of its old town with lanes full of corners and the gothic cathedral of St-Siffrein with a small treasury. Also of interest is the Inguimbertine library with its many old books.

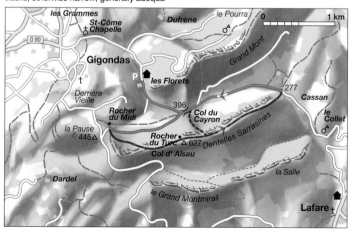

The bizarre white rock pinnacles of the Dentelles Sarrasines.

Despite its low height, this walk offers extensive views and the bizarre white pinnacles, the colour of which contrasts strongly with the blue of the sky and the green of the mountain slopes.

From the **car park** go along the forest road at first concrete and steep, then dusty but easy-going to the **Col du Cayron** (396m: 10 min: splendid views of the Dentelles). At the pass take the forest road on the right, which is almost level and leads westwards. It is very sunny and offers a good distant view of the Rhone, over Mont Ventoux to the Vaucluse Plateau. After 20 minutes the **Rocher du Midi** (about 450m) is reached.

Here a narrow path with blue waymarkings branches off to the Dentelles Sarrasines. Follow this path, which rises steadily, but not too-steeply through green bushes. The imposing rock pinnacles draw nearer and the view expands. After the ascent the dusty and rocky path leads with slight up and downhill sections along the north base of the cliffs. Two gaps offer views to the south, and the **Rocher du Turc**, the highest point is reached (about 600m).

At a fork in the path (50 min from the Rocher du Midi) do not take the left direct descent path to the Col du Cayron (see alternative) but rather the path with blue waymarkings, which continues to the right below the Dentelles. At first this leads on without any great drop in height, but at the height of Deves the path drops steeply to a vineyard and at the edge of this reaches a dusty forest road(**P. 227m**; 40 min). This goes upwards slightly to the left back to the **Col du Cayron** and the **car park** (30 min).

10 La Grande Montagne

The panoramic high ridge opposite the Dentelles de Montmirail

Les Florets – Pas de l'Aigle – Grande Montagne – les Florets

Location: Carpentras, 102m.
Starting point: From Carpentras drive as for walk 9 to the car park at les Florets (350m), 17km from Carpentras.
Walking time: Les Florets – Pas de l'Aigle: 1¼ hrs; Pas de l'Aigle – Grande Montagne – les Florets: 1½ hrs; total time: 2¾ hrs.
Ascent: About 350m.
Highest point: 594m at the Grande Montagne.
Grade: Walk along minor roads and rocky paths which require sure-footedness; the

waymarkings are adequate, so there should not be any route-finding difficulties.
Alternative: If you are not put off by the poor gravelled road it is possible to drive to the Col du Cayron and so shorten the walk by 15 min. Walks 9 and 10 also offer the possibility of a combined walk of 5 hrs.
Places of Interest: The small town of Séguret to the north, which is situated like an eagle's eyri, has a mediaeval old town, a Romanesque church and fine views.

The walk leads through the varied hilly country of the North Provence and offers fine views of the rock pinnacles of the Dentelles de Montmirail and Mont Ventoux with its light scree covered top.

From the **car park** go up to the **Col du Cayron** (see walk 9). Cross the broad saddle to the east and at each of the next two forks take the left track with red waymarkings. The path mainly leads on the level or gently downhill through open forest with pine trees and garrigue vegetation. Repeatedly there are wonderful views of the bizarre white rock needles of the Dentelles de Mont-

From the Pas de l'Aigle the view stretches far to the north.

mirail, the summit veil of Mont Ventoux, whose limestone scree appears from a distance to be snow, and the Crête de St-Amand. After a short uphill section there is a longer downhill stretch. The path turns gradually to the northeast and the Dentelles disappear from sight. The path goes above a vineyard and on up to a saddle with a fork. Take the left-hand road (blue waymarkings), which shortly after has a right-hand bend and a little later offers a beautiful view to the north. This point is named the **Pas de l'Aigle** (wooden sign; a good hr) although the actual pass is somewhat lower to the right. Go back a few metres along the same path and now take the yellow waymarked path on the right before the saddle (notice board). Now go up through a wood to the ridge of the **Grande Montagne** (594m). Follow the various rises on the ridge with even better views than on the lower path (585m, 565m) and at any branches follow the yellow waymarkings (on the right). Now go down slightly and go for a distance more easily through scrub to reach a rocky path which goes down more steeply. After this the path goes continually up and down on the ridge, sometimes in open forest, sometimes with a splendid view of the Dentelles, Mont Ventoux and the Crête de St-Amand until a final col with views is reached. Now it finally goes downhill and in the scrub it gets progressively steeper. At two forks follow the yellow markings on the left and after a final steep descent reach the road, which is already familiar from the approach walk. Go along this (right) via the **Col du Cayron** back to the **car park** (1½ hrs).

11 Notre-Dame-d'Aubune

Landscape and vines, culture and ruins at Beaumes-de-Venise

Notre-Dame-d'Aubune – Beaumes-de-Venise – Château de Durban – Notre Dame-d'Aubune

Location: Carpentras, 102m.

Starting point: From Carpentras drive along the wide D 7 via Aubignan to the north and shortly after the junction with the D 81 turn right (signpost is small) along the narrow tarmac road in the direction of Notre-Dame-d'Aubune (110m; 10km from Carpentras). There are only a few places to park at the chapel, but there are places to park in Beaumes-de-Venise.

Walking time: Notre-Dame-d'Aubune – Beaumes-de-Venise: 30 min; Beaumes-de-Venise – Château de Durban: 1 hr; Château de Durban – Notre-Dame-d'Aubune: 45 min; total time: 2¼ hrs.

Ascent: good 200m.

Highest point: About 250m on the ridge above Beaumes-de-Venise.

Grade: Easy walking on tracks (short section with no track) and minor roads. As there is a lack of waymarking, navigation could be difficult if care is not taken.

Refreshments: Bars in Beaumes-de-Venise.

A varied walk with changes in vegetation, beautiful views, a well-known wine area and places of cultural interest.

From the Romanesque **chapel** go back along the minor, metalled approach road to the south to a canal. Cross the canal and then turn off left and go along a track on the bank. At the next junction cross the canal again (towards the left) and immediately turn right into a road that leads from the chapel to Beaumes (faint, blue-yellow waymarkings). Go through vineyards with a view of a ruin, the chapel behind you and the steep slopes on the left to reach the wine town of **Beaumes-de-Venise**. There, take a turning down to the right to the main road (D 21) and then continue left to the main square (30 min). Here take the left fork, along a road, which goes past the church through an arch

The idyllically-situated Chapel of Notre-Dame-d'Aubune.

(from here called Rue de la République), which leads to the Place de la Liberté. Now go right up the Rue de Presbytère, through another arch to the Place du Portail neuf, which has a small fountain. Immediately after this leave the town via some steps on the left. After this first stage the walk continues to the right up over steps to a water tank. To the left of this is the cliff top castle of Beaumes. The path goes down for a short way to a field and meets a tarmac road at a point between vines and power lines. Follow the road to the left, staying on it beyond the end of the asphalt. After a left-hand bend go straight on, and shortly after a barrier take a yellow-marked path on the right (almost 30 min) which leads up the slope to a vineyard which is followed to the right. After 50 metres take a path in a westerly direction, turning off right at the next fork. The panoramic high path offers extensive views over the Ouvèze Valley. At an olive grove below a ruin go down to the left over walled terrases to a path at right angles. Follow this path uphill to the right to the ruins of the **Château de Durban** which can already be seen (good 30 min). Here go left along the top of the hill past vineyards to the ruin of the Romanesque Chapel of St-Hilaire. Stay on the high path on the edge of the ridge and reach the so-called »devil's rock«, a prominent block (a red-yellow waymarked spur path leads in a few minutes to the Grottes d'Ambrosi). Now go straight on via the red-yellow waymarked path, which soon steepens and descends in zigzags over a stony slope with garrigue vegetation. Shortly above **Notre-Dame-d'Aubune** the approach road is reached (go right here) to the chapel (45 min).

12 Combe de Curnier

A little-known unspoilt gorge on the south slope of Mont Ventoux

Les Fébriers – Combe de Curnier – Jas des Landérots – les Fébriers

Location: Carpentras, 102m.

Starting point: From Carpentras drive along the D 974 via Bédoin in the direction of Mont Ventoux and turn off for les Baux before Ste-Colombe. There keep right all the time and take the Chemin de Fébriers to the houses of the same name, where sufficient parking spaces are to be found on the side of the road at the end of the asphalt at a large crossing (506m), 20km from Carpentras.

Walking time: Les Fébriers – Combe de Curnier – Jas des Landérots: 2 hrs; Jas des Landérots – les Fébriers: 1½ hrs; total time: 3½ hrs.

Ascent: About. 570m.

Highest point: 1021m at Jas des Landérots.

Grade: On the whole a sufficiently well-marked path, which did not ought to cause any navigation difficulties. However, sure-footedness is required especially in the gorge parts (no exposed sections).

Alternative: If you are in a hurry, instead of climbing up the red waymarked path, you can follow the same waymarkings along a stony road that leads directly towards the valley through open scrub vegetation and with views towards Luberon, as far as the GR 91, from which you go back left to the starting point (45 min).

Advice: The gorge should under all circumstances be avoided after heavy rain or during a thunderstorm.

Places of Interest: Bédoin: a small town on

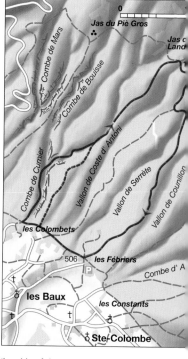

the side of the mountain with picturesque lanes.

The walk goes through an unspoilt little-known gorge and open scrub on the south slopes of Mont Ventoux offering impressive views towards the Luberon mountain chain.

The steep rock walls in the Combe de Curnier appear almost off-putting.

The unknown hamlet of les Baux on the sunny south slopes of Mont Ventoux.

From **les Fébriers** take the red and white marked GR 91 on the left (westerly direction), which goes between open woods and fields on the extreme south edge of Mont Ventoux. This leads slightly downhill (interrupted by some short uphill sections) to les Colombets farmhouse (about 450m; 15 min). At this point turn right onto a stony path, which initially has blue waymarkings (later also yellow signs), and continuously follows the base of the **Combe de Curnier**. At first it winds with little ascent through the sparsely vegetated gorge, although at some points bushes make the path narrow. Then comes the most impressive, somewhat steeper section: high cliffs, narrow sections, often only wide enough for one person and with caves gouged out by the water. After this stretch the valley widens again and the stony path leads very steeply out of the gorge. At this point there is a minor road at right angles, which is followed for a few minutes to the right (i.e. in the opposite direction). Then the forest road is left (690m; 45 min) and a red waymarked footpath is followed, which leads steadily uphill in the original direction through open forest (some cedars, many beech trees, and the typical evergreen garrigue vegetation). Keep following the red markings, with an occasional view back to the Vaucluse plateau and the Luberon, to reach the **Jas des Landérots** (1021m; 1 hr) an old alpine meadow on the western ridge of the Vallon de Coste d'Antoni. Here the red-white waymarked GR 91 B is reached, which is followed slightly downhill for a short time to the right. At a height of about 980m take a yellow-marked path to the right, which leads southwards towards the valley. After about 500m the markings lead off to the left (straight on is a parallel path in the valley direction). Go a little way to the east and then go south again to go downhill on the ridge between Vallon de Serrète (west) and Vallon de Counillon (east). There are repeated views of the Vaucluse Plateau with the Luberon in the background. Keep following the yellow waymarkings to arrive again at **les Fébriers** after 1½ hours of varied walking.

Pine trees offer pleasant shade (at les Fébriers).

13 Forest and gorges of Venasque

Thick forests and deep gorges on the Vaucluse Plateau

Camp Long – Fontaine du Rupt – la Nauque – Camp Long

Location: Carpentras, 102m.

Starting point: From Carpentras drive along the D 4 in the direction of Apt, past Venasque. About 3km after Venasque just before a sharp left-hand bend watch out for a sign for the access road to the Gîte »Borel« (320m). There are virtually no public parking places there. However, if you ask the friendly owner of the gîte, he will certainly allow you to use his private parking for the duration of the walk (14km from Carpentras).

Walking time: Camp Long – 1st turning / Vaucluse Plateau: 1½ hrs; 1st turning – Junction with GR: 1¼ hrs; GR junction – Camp Long: 1 hr; total time: 3¾ hrs.

Ascent: About 380m.

Highest point: About 560m on the Vaucluse Plateau.

Grade: Mainly adequately marked walking track which is somewhat rocky and over-grown; the sections in the gorge require sure-footedness, although there are no particularly exposed sections.

Places of Interest: The old town of Venasque situated on a steep cliff possesses one of the oldest buildings in France – a Merovingian baptistery (believed to be 6th century).

This walk impresses with its variation from beautiful forest sections to wild gorges and far-reaching views. With luck one can even see wild boar.

From the private car parking at the **gîte** go back to the approach road and turn right there (yellow marking). The track leads gently down a valley where it is necessary to take a second path to the right with yellow markings (new sign). The path leads easily into a shady oak forest and therefore only allows occasional glimpses back to Mont Ventoux. After about 20 minutes turn off into the unspoilt gorge of Combe de Cambredon. The stony, gently rising path leads through open vegetation; breath-taking scenery and beautiful downward views dominate the picture. At the end the path, which is very steep and covered in stones, leads out of the gorge to reach its highest point on the **Vaucluse Plateau** (about 560m; 50 min). After a slight up and down

The gorge of Fontaine du Rupt with Mont Ventoux in the background.

section a second oak wood is passed as well as a small valley and a pine forest. 20 minutes later the yellow waymarkings fork off to the right and shortly after lead leftwards to the edge of the plateau. Now walk down a steep and stony path through a wood into the gorge of **Combe de la Fontaine du Rupt**. At the bottom follow the yellow markings gently to the right down to the valley. The path is partly overgrown by thorny tough-leaved bushes. After 30 minutes go up a rocky, sunny slope with beautiful views of Mont Ventoux out of the gorge to a col with fine views, from where the route continues gently down to a track (30 min). Follow this straight on (yellow markings) and after 15 minutes reach the red-white marked GR 91, which leads rightwards through a small oak wood to the **la Nauque** farmhouse. From here take the tarmac road, which leads steeply to the bottom of the valley. Shortly after the asphalt finishes the GR turns off to the right (Board: »Camp Long«; about 260m). At a field it is necessary to watch out for the markings – the continuation is more or less without a path on the right edge of the field. After that the path goes slightly uphill through a forested gorge to a short steep section which leads out of the gorge. The path continues past fields and vineyards back to the starting point at **Camp Long** (1 hr).

14 In the Forest of St-Lambert

Solitude on a quiet wooded plateau

St-Hubert – Pas du Viguier – Indochinois Forest track – Fillol – St-Hubert

Location: Sault, 765m in the Nesque Valley.
Starting point: From Sault drive along the D 943 to the south and after 10km take the narrow but tarmac D 5 (right) which leads to the St-Hubert Gîte d'étape (about 850m) where it is possible to park on the side of the road, 15km from Sault.
Walking time: St-Hubert – RF des Indochinois: good 1¼ hrs; RF des Indochinois – Fillol: 1¼ hrs; Fillol – St-Hubert: almost 1½ hrs; total time: 4 hrs.
Ascent: About. 250m.
Highest Point: Pas du Viguier (about 870m).
Grade: Not particularly strenuous walking

on generally marked paths or small roads, but the walk does require some attention to directions.
Alternative: If you miss the turning off from the GR 91 A, you can continue to the D 5. There go left and then left again onto the D 15 as far as the Indochinois forest track and then left again until it leads onto the normal route. The alternative is less beautiful and about 1km longer.
Places of Interest: The town of Sault, built on top of a crag, is a centre for the lavender industry, and in addition to a small archaeological museum, it has an old church with a beautiful Romanesque nave.

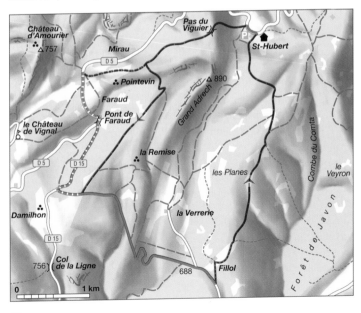

Flowering thistles in the peaceful forest of St-Lambert (Vaucluse Plateau).

The pleasant walk through the large forest area of the Vaucluse Plateau with its rich vegetation offers peace and seclusion and has some fine views of Mont Ventoux. It is a route for individualists.

From the **St-Hubert** Gîte d'étape take the red and white marked GR 91 A, which goes up gently through an allée in a westerly direction to the **Pas du Viguier** (about 870m). Now the path loses a good 100 metres of height and after half an hour it is necessary to watch out. Leave the GR (about 760m) and take a narrow path to the left (marked red-orange/ 2 yellow dots), which winds its way up to a ridge (about 810m). From here the path continues with a slight downwards tendency. This pleasant high path, which is lined by beautiful oaks has especially good views and after about 45 minutes leads to the **Route Forestière des Indochinois** (about 750m), which is followed in an easterly direction. The narrow, tarmac but, nevertheless, hardly-used forest road first drops slightly then more steeply through the forest of St-Lambert. At the junction of a spur track from La Verrerie (left) the lowest point is passed (688m). Shortly after turn left onto the metalled spur track, which leads to the Fillol farmhouse (about 700m; 1¼ hrs). Before **Fillol** take a yellow-marked path on the right with a sign to »St-Hubert«. It first goes slightly upwards over a clear space in an open wood, then even sections alternate with short uphill stretches, so that there is a steady, if slight, gain in height. Only towards the end does the path drop slightly to **St-Hubert**, which is situated a little to the right of the path. After nearly 1½ hours, the starting point is reached again.

15 Gorges de la Nesque

Even the poet, Mistral, sang the praises of this unspoilt, forbidding-looking gorge

Plan d'Eau – Monieux – Savournin – D 942 – St-Michel – Plan d'Eau

Location: Sault, 765m in the Nesque Valley.
Starting point: From Sault drive along the

wide D 942 down the valley to Monieux. At the end of the town turn off left and go along a minor metalled road to the Plan d'Eau (623m) which has a gîte d'étape and a spacious car park, 7km from Sault.

Walking time: Plan d'Eau – Monieux/GR: 30 min; Monieux – D 942: good 1¼ hrs; D 942 – GR turning off: 45 min; GR turning off – Plan d'Eau: 55 min; total time: 3½ hrs.

Ascent: About. 360m.

Highest point: 859m at Savournin.

Grade: Short road section, otherwise marked tracks or paths, sometimes steep, which therefore require sure-footedness, a head for heights and fitness.

Refreshments: Restaurants in Monieux.

Alternative: From Savournin it is possible to take a small, unmarked path, which goes straight on and later joins the GR. It takes somewhat less time.

Places of Interest: The panoramic D 942 from Sault to Carpentras, which runs high above the gorge, offers an impressive outing. There are signposted viewpoints, which offer fascinating views into the depths of the gorge (especially of the 400m high Rocher du Cire, the walls of which are punctured with caves).

A small stream, generally dry in summer, has created the most impressive gorge of the Vaucluse Plateau, whose walls tower up to 400 metres in height. At only two points does the path lead into the mainly inaccessible bottom of the gorge, but at various points it offers breath-taking views into the depths. From the **car park** go along the approach road slightly uphill to **Monieux (about** 20 min: 652m) and along the D 942 into the town. Here take a small street on the left, that becomes a path beyond the last houses, and follow this, still without any markings, to the right past a house until after about 200m it reaches the red-white marked GR 9 (10 min). Follow this to the left, quickly gaining height on a steep section on the slopes of Côte Renard and obtaining frequent glimpses into the mighty Nesque Gorge. After a more

The 400m high Rocher du Cire above the Gorges de la Nesque.

level section one should watch out not to miss the marked left fork of the GR at a largish bush (45 min). Keep following the waymarkings to reach the highest point of the walk (about 859m). Ignore an unmarked path to the left, and go slightly leftwards at the **Savournin** farmhouse. The path now goes through a varied landscape, finally in long drawn-out zigzags down to the **D 942** (739m; 35 min). After crossing the road the marked GR 9 descends steeply in zigzags and over steps down into the base of the **Gorges de la Nesque** with the **St-Michel** chapel (15 min) picturesquely situated at the stream under a cliff. Cross the stream (about 600m), then the red-white waymarked path leads in steep zigzags back out of the gorge and goes along the top of a vertical rock wall (take care!). After reaching the edge of the gorge a pleasant stretch of track leads to a fork (about 700m; 30 min). Now leave the GR 9 and take the track with yellow/orange waymarks. This leads on pleasantly, shaded in parts, and offers beautiful backward views of the rock walls of the Rocher du Cire. Now it continues with two steeper downhill sections interrupted by a level section. There are only infrequent views of the gorge. After the second downhill stretch, the valley bottom is reached again, where there is usually only a small stream. The rare Phoenician juniper grows here. It is only 10 minutes along the stream bank through the delightful gorge before the rocks suddenly disappear and the **car park** is reached (just 1 hr from the GR).

16 Gorges du Gardon

Clear water and light-coloured rock

Collias – Chapelle St-Vérédème and back

Location: Uzès, 138m.

Starting point: From Uzès drive along the D 981 in the direction of Avignon and turn right after 7km onto the D 3, which is followed to Collias, (43m; 10km from Uzès). Park there on the left bank of the river (boat hire) where the gorge begins.

Walking time: Collias – St-Vérédème: good 1½ hrs; Return route: a little under 1½ hrs; total time: 3 hrs.

Ascent: Negligible.

Highest point: St-Vérédème, about 55m.

Grade: Well marked track in valley without particular difficulties, not even on a short, rope-protected section, although the ascent to the chapel does require some care.

Alternative: For anyone, who, despite the beauty of the landscape, does not want to return via the same route, there is an alternative. At the stone dam go right up the slope along a path, which is steep in places, following light-red waymarkings, which are not always clear. Go left at the first fork, right at a cave, pass a first junction and take the first left at a second one, then immediately right again. The red-white waymarked GR 6 A is reached on the plateau and is taken in an easterly direction (right) through garrigue landscape to Collias, going right at the main square down to the river (about 2 hrs; 120 metres of height gain).

Places of Interest: 8km downstream is found the Pont du Gard, a giant Roman aqueduct from the time shortly after 19 AD, which crosses the Gardon at a height of 49m and with a span of 275m in three levels.

The walk leads through shady forest, dense scrub and over light-coloured limestone rocks, always accompanied by the clear, blue-green Gardon, which has created an impressive gorge here. Today the gorge is a nature reserve both on account of its beauty and its rare plants and animals.

From the **car park** go upstream to the entrance of the gorge where there is a nature reserve information board and then follow the continuous red-white GR 6 waymarkings. After a few metres there is a locked cave on the right.

High, almost vertical cliffs enclose the valley, on the slopes of which cactus grow, which come into flower in spring. Along the continuation of the path, in addition to interesting rock formations, one can see frogs, snakes, butterflies (e.g. swallowtails) preying mantis, beavers, bats and birds of prey, as well as unusual plants. At first the path leads through a shady forest with rich vegetation, then it continues over stone slabs, mainly along the river to the Roche Tombée (a huge rock which has fallen out of the gorge wall). Here there is a narrow, but not dangerous, section (about 1m above the river), which is protected by a rope. Then it continues mainly through dense shrubs. After nearly 1½ hrs, a small stone dam is reached; on the opposite side the ruins and the approach road to la Baume can be glimpsed. Here it is necessary to watch out, for beyond the dam there is a small path on the right which leads in a few minutes up the slope to the **St-Vérédème** chapel (about 55 m). From here there is a fine view over the valley of the Gardon.

The best way back is along the same path, as the gorge, sometimes charming, sometimes wild and rugged, can be seen from a completely different perspective.

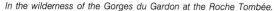

In the wilderness of the Gorges du Gardon at the Roche Tombée.

17 St-Michel-de-Frigolet

Along shady paths through a splendid pine forest to an abbey

Barbentane – St-Michel-de-Frigolet – Barbentane

Location: Tarascon, 9m.

Starting point: From Tarascon drive along the minor D 35 to the north as far as Barbentane. At the entrance to the town take the D 35 E, which leads to a car park on the right (40m) just outside the town, 15km from Tarascon.

Walking time: Barbentane – St-Michel: 1½ hrs; Back to Barbentane: 1¼ hrs; total time: 2¾ hrs.

Ascent: Insignificant.

Highest point: St-Michel-de-Frigolet, 101m.

Grade: Easy walk along shady tracks without any significant exertion. The number of paths and tracks can be a bit confusing; if you keep going in a southerly direction you should reach the destination.

Alternative: One of the many side paths.

Advice: Not recommended on Sundays because of the number of people.

Places of Interest: While in the Abbey of St-Michel it is only the chapel of N.-D.-du-Bon-Remède (11th cent) with its wooden panellings (1683), which is worth seeing, Barbentane has a beautiful castle (17th cent) with rich interior furnishings (18th cent). In Tarascon the mighty castle (15th cent) and the Romanesque church of Ste-Marthe (12th cent) are worth a visit.

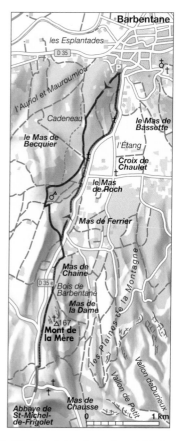

A shady path leads through the hilly country of Montagnette, which is covered by a large pine forest, to a much-visited place of pilgrimage, which on weekdays offers both peace and natural beauty.

One of the many forest paths to the Abbey of St-Michel-de-Frigolet.

Many paths lead to Rome and also to St-Michel-de-Frigolet: there are numerous paths, with the most varied markings, and for which there is no information board. From the **car park** go right immediately to the left of an estate along a shady path in the beautiful pine forest and follow red, yellow or red-white-red waymarkings. In doing so, and this is very important, keep to a southerly direction and take note of the not too-distant noise from the approach road to the abbey. Go along the wide track, very slightly uphill, until the approach road is crossed after a good hour, between km 3.5 and 4. Then follow the marked path to the abbey through open woodland just left of the road. After 1½ hrs (from the car park) at the end of the road the abbey of **St-Michel-de-Frigolet** (101m) is reached and it is possible to add on a visit. For the return section, first follow the same route as on the approach. After crossing the D 35 E it is recommended, partly because finding the way is easier, to take the first path which leads down to the west parallel to the road through the pine forest, so that the road is kept in view or within earshot. This leads without route-finding difficulties back to the **car park** (1¼ hrs).

18 Gorges de Véroncle

A narrow gorge with remains of old water mills

Les Grailles – Gorges de Véroncle – Murs – Bois d'Audibert – les Grailles

Location: Apt, 222m in the Calavon Valley.
Starting point: From Apt first take the N 100 to the west and then the D 4 to the north until the minor D 2 turns off to the left. After a good 5km on this road turn right onto a road which is un-metalled with a sign to the »Gorges de Véroncle« and park about 500m further on at the side of the road (about 210m), 17km from Apt.
Walking time: 2½ hrs through the gorge to Murs; From Murs to les Grailles via the Bois d'Audibert: 2 hrs; total time: 4½ hrs.
Ascent: About 300m.
Highest point: Murs (501m).
Grade: The path through the gorge requires sure-footedness and an iron ladder demands a head for heights as well, but the path is well marked. The rest of the walk is not difficult, although some attention to navigation is required.
Refreshment: Numerous possibilities in Murs.
Places of Interest: To the west of the gorge

the Romanesque Cistercian abbey of Sénanque is worth visiting. The church, cloister and monastery buildings impress with their simple architecture. Very nearby is the picturesque little hillside town of Gordes, with its narrow alleys and old houses, which is situated on side of a hill. A bit further afield there are the well-known Borries: hive-shaped stone huts between 200 and 500 years old.

The contrast-rich walk leads at first through the unspoilt, nowadays dried-out Véroncles gorge, with its former mills and goes through the beautiful Audibert pine forest on the way back.

Follow the signpost to the gorge from the road in **les Grailles**. The waymarked path (at first yellow, later blue) leads at first somewhat above the **Véroncle** and later down to the valley bottom, which since the earthquake in 1887 is practically without water. Consequently numerous trees and shrubs have established themselves. At the first mill, go up the slope to the left. The most difficult section follows, for the path leads over a rock band above the gorge. After crossing the streambed, there is an ascent of the rock face by means of a ladder about 5m long. This is followed by another exposed section (rope protection) and a crossing of the gorge. This is the wildest section of the narrow canyon with many cascades and deep pools; steeper sections alternate with level parts. The gorge continues to be quite narrow: many deep pools line this romantic section of path, which leads past the remnants of many flour mills, still in use into the 19th century. After, the gorge gradually widens and the slopes are covered in the typical garrigue vegetation of the Vaucluse Plateau. At the last mill, the Moulin des Étangs (414m), the gorge comes to an end after 1¾ hrs. Now cross a stone bridge and pass the remains of an earlier reservoir dam. Along a grass-covered area a path is reached and then a small tarmac road, which leads gradually uphill to **Murs**

Iron ladder in the enchanted Gorge de Véroncle at the trickiest part of the walk.

(501m; 45 min). There take the D 4 to the right (direction of Apt) and go straight on in a left-hand bend along a level tarred road for 20 minutes to a holiday village (sign: »Village de vacances«). Keep right here, then left (the right goes to Les Chalottes). Go past a campsite, going straight on at the end of it on a forest track which is almost level at the beginning. Stay on this wide track, ignoring any turnings off. The track leads through the wonderful **Bois d'Audibert** steadily downwards in wide curves to les Cortasses. On reaching the level (1½ hrs) turn left at a junction (straight on goes to les Cortasses) to reach the starting point at **les Grailles** via a level path with blue waymarkings (10 min).

19 Roussillon

A picturesque little town and brightly-coloured ochre cliffs

St-Joseph – Roussillon – Chaussée des Géants – St-Joseph

Location: Apt, 222m in the Calavon Valley.
Starting point: From Apt first drive along the N 100 and then go onto the D 4 in a westerly

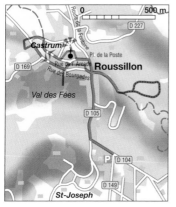

/ north-westerly direction until a left-hand turn into the narrow D 104. At the crossroads with the D 149 (296m) it is possible to park on the side of the road, 10km from Apt. (In Roussillon all parking is metered.)

Walking time: Approach and return route: About 45 min; Circuit in the town: About 45 min; Walk through the ochre quarries: About 45 min; total time: about 2¼ hrs.

Ascent: Good 100m.

Highest point: 390m at Castrum.

Grade: Narrow lanes and tracks present no problems; sure-footedness needed in the ochre quarries. Keep to the paths there and observe the warning notices: the rock is crumbly and after rain it is slippery.

Refreshments: Numerous restaurants in the town.

Places of interest: 4km to the south the Roman bridge »Pont Julien« over the Calavon (built 3 BC) can be admired.

The small town of Roussillon is picturesquely situated on a rock plateau, has charming old alleyways and offers beautiful views. The high point is the splendidly-coloured ochre rocks in the green coniferous forest.

From the **car park** first continue westwards along the D 104 and then take the D 105 on the right through a thick coniferous forest. The first ochre-coloured rocks can already be admired on both sides of the road. After about 25 minutes the main square in **Roussillon** is reached. At the far end of the Place de la Poste turn left into the Rue Casteau, a narrow shopping lane in the old town. At the Place de la Mairie one can make a detour to the north (right) to get an initial view from the Place Mathieu. Otherwise go on right under the clock tower and up the Rue de l'Église past the church to Castrum. From the platform (orientation table) above the rocks there is a view into the distance to the north over the Vaucluse Plateau to Mont Ventoux and towards the south to the Luberon. Now go right, past the church on the edge of the rocks down over the Forge and Pignotte squares and then right into the Rue Jeu de Paume. From here there are some good views over the ochre cliffs to the south. Leave the town down the Rue de l'Heureuse, and then go left to follow the ring road (D 169). Follow this to the left around the cliffs into the

Red-brown impressions in the Roussillon ochre cliffs.

town and then go straight on along the narrow Rue des Bourgades. After the Rue des Lauriers (left) turn right into a narrow little lane, from the end of which there is a wonderful view of the ochre-coloured pinnacles of the Val des Fées. Now go back along the same route via the Rue des Lauriers (now on the right) to the Place de l'Abbé Avon. After that go up the steps of the Rue de l'Arcade, a picturesque lane to the Rue des Bourgades. Then go right over the Place du Pasquier to the Avenue de la Burlière (about 45 min). Now go right and then immediately left up to the **Chaussée des Géants**, where during the day it is necessary to pay for a visit. There, go along the marked circuit (about 45 min), which should not be left as the ground drops away and there is a danger of landslips. The walk goes downhill and offers fascinating views of the bizarre rock pinnacles and earth pyramids of the **ochre quarries** with almost 20 different shades of colour, which contrast strongly with the green of the conifers and holm oaks growing on the slopes. In the woods at the foot of the cliffs a small stream is reached which is the turning point for the walk. Before turning left into the Avenue de la Burlière, you should take a look at the view of Rousillon from the viewing platform. Go along the above-mentioned road, classified as the D 105 (then D 104), which, after about 20 minutes, leads back to the starting point.

20 The Colorado of Rustrel

Fantastic rock formations in many shades of ochre

Bouvène – Cheminées des Fées – Cirque de Barriès – Sahara – Bouvène

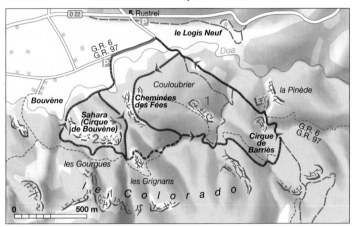

Location: Apt, 222m in the Calavon Valley.
Starting point: From Apt take the D 22 in the direction of Rustrel, but rather than driving into the town turn right onto a narrow metalled road in the direction of Bouvène/Colorado. After a left fork the guarded car park with a small kiosk is reached (about 360m, parking charge) About 12km from Apt.
Walking time: Bouvène – Cheminées des Fées: 30 min; Cheminées des Fées – Junction with the GR 6: 1 hr; GR 6 – car park: 30 min; (time for 1st loop: 2 hrs); Car park – cascade: almost 30 min; cascade – car park: 1 hr; (time for 2nd loop: almost 1½ hrs); total time: almost 3½ hrs.
Ascent: about 150m in total.
Highest point: About 450m at Cirque de Barriès.

Grade: The first loop of the walk requires some sure-footedness and a head for heights; the second is completely unproblematic. Waymarkings are excellent on both sections.
Alternative: Between the two loops, which can be done individually there is a more direct, connecting path (also marked) which goes left up the hill from the waterfall to join the other path between Cheminées des Fées and Cirque de Barriès: walking time depending on the route, between 1½ and 2 hrs.
Advice: Make sure that you take note of the warning on the notice board and keep the necessary distance from the edges of the slopes as the rock is very crumbly and the ground is subject to landslides. Bad accidents have occurred.

The walk takes in the most beautiful part of the Provençale Colorado, which is not actually a gorge, but rather owes its name to the various shades of colour in the ochre quarries. Through the extraction of the rock by man and the effect of erosion a bizarre landscape has been created with colours to enthuse any photographer.

From the **car park** continue along the minor tarmac road for about 5 minutes in an easterly direction until the red and white marked GR 6 to Doa leads down to a ford, which is crossed on slippery stones. This can be problematic after heavy rain; moreover mosquitoes can also be a real plague. Immediately after the stream the green-marked path goes off to the right and leads steeply up into a shady wood. After the uphill

Earth pyramids in the Colorado of Rustrel.

section the level path offers repeated beautiful views of the ochre rocks with their numerous glowing red and yellow tones. After 30 minutes the viewpoint (belvédère) at the **Cheminées des Fées** is reached, the view from which is strongly reminiscent of an earth pyramid. Shortly after there are also views down into the depths of the valley of the Cirque de Bouvène. Continue to follow the green markings (on the right the connection to the Sahara forks off) between low bushes and shrubs to the high ridge. After a dip and a narrow section, which leads uphill over slippery rocks, the path continues along the quarries of the **Cirque de Barriès** until after a further hour of mainly level ground the wide GR 6 is reached. Turn off left here and follow the wide, red and white marked track, which leads steadily but without difficulty back to the valley with beautiful views of the Cirque de Barriès. At the Doa the path meets the approach path again and after 30 min the **car park** is reached. Here follow the white waymarkings downstream along the Doa and cross the stream again. In the shady wood follow the left-hand path with the white markings, which passes a water pipe, and after 30 minutes reaches the end of the path at a small, picturesque waterfall. Go back here and follow the white markings, which immediately lead left to the **Sahara**. The path leads over this bare area along the edge of the quarries of the Cirque de Bouvène, offering fantastic views of the varied blaze of colours of the ochre quarries. There is then a right-hand bend in the path and it leads between the Sahara and the Doa until it meets the approach path, which leads to the left back to the **car park** (1 hr).

21 Gorges de Regalon

Through the narrowest gorge in the Provence

La Tuillère – Gorges de Regalon – St-Phalès – Mérindol – la Tuillère

Location: Cavaillon, 75m in the Durance Valley.

Starting point: From Cavaillon drive up the valley for about 13.5km eastwards along the D 973 and then turn left and follow signs to the gorge as far as the car park at la Tuillère (about 120m), 14km from Cavaillon.

Walking time: Car park – St-Phalès: 1¼ hrs: St-Phalès – Vieux Mérindol: 1¼ hrs; Mérindol – Car park: 1½ hrs; total time: 4 hrs.

Ascent: About 350m.

Highest point: 336m at the Sommet du Vallon Bernard.

Grade: Mainly satisfactory, marked tracks, in parts on tarmac; the last part does however require a sense of direction. The

path through the gorge demands surefootedness and involves easy scrambling.

Refreshments: A short detour allows various refreshment options in Mérindol.

Alternative: If you have any difficulties with route finding on the final part of the walk, it is also possible to go south to the D 973 and follow that back to the car park (2km).

Advice: Early in the year or after heavy rain the gorge is not passable as the stream then has water in it.

Places of Interest: Cavaillon has several churches and a small, interesting archaeological museum. A worthwhile detour (15km to the north) takes one to the beautiful stalactite caves of Thouzon.

The Gorges de Regalon is the narrowest and darkest gorge in the Provence. Because of the plentiful vegetation and prehistoric significance it enjoys special protection. The rest of the walk leads through a varied landscape and takes in a viewpoint.

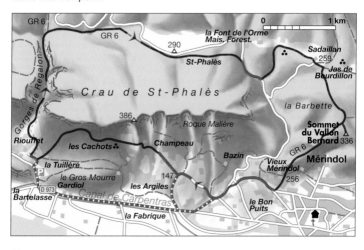

From the **carpark,** go along the blue-marked path, past cultivated fields and olive trees, to the nearby entrance to the gorge. The route stays in the streambed of the **Gorges de Regalon** and on account of the nature reserve this must be kept to. It is very shady and at times it is necessary to climb over boulders, but this does not present any problems. The rich flora is impressive, especially pines, holm oaks, pistachio trees, ivy and Phoenician juniper. First of all go through thick scrub into the gorge. On the sides there are caves, which are indicative of a prehistoric settlement. After a short tunnel – a torch is useful here – comes the most impressive section. Here the Regalon has gouged out a gorge from the surrounding limestone – up to 40 metres high, but in parts only 1 metre wide. Towards the end of the gorge comes the unpleasant part. On a slippery, slightly overhanging rock with few footholds it is necessary to scramble up about 2 metres. The steadily-rising path now has a wooded stretch, which is followed until the GR 6 is reached (30 minutes). The red and white markings of this lead along the upper reach of the Regalon. Elder, box and sycamore trees line the shady path, which goes up slightly between cliffs. On the edge of the Crau de St-Phalès, a cultivated plateau (especially vines), a road is met, which is followed to the east over level ground to the **St-Phalès** farmhouse (290m; 45 min). Here turn right onto the GR. A bit further on the two paths, which lead slightly downwards, join up again. At the next junction leave the road to the left, follow a bit more asphalt, go round a crest and meet the estate of Sadaillan (259m; 40 min). Shortly after the GR branches off to the right and becomes a little steeper. A short detour leads to the **Sommet du Vallon Bernard (**336m), the highest point of a bare hill, which allows fine prospects of the Durance Valley in the direction of the sea. The marked path now leads downhill again and after 35 minutes comes to the ruins of the **Vieux Mérindol** (256m) on the right. After a few minutes a small road is reached where the GR turns off to the left for Mérindol. Carry on to the right. At the next junction, keep to the right, and then go immediately to the left again. At the following larger fork take a large bend to the right and at the next junction go along the Chemin de Champeau to the right where the road ends at a farmhouse of the same name (about 150m; 45 min). Go through the houses and almost immediately take a road to the left, which goes up in a north-westerly direction along the valley slopes, passing the ruins of Cachot. After a final rise the path slopes down more steeply through a wood. At a junction stay to the right along a meadow and then right along a wide path at right angles, where the familiar olive groves from the approach walk are met. From here go a short distance to the south to the starting-point (45 min).

22 The Cedar Forest of the Petit Luberon

Two panoramic loops through the cedar forest and along the summit ridge

Massif des Cèdres car park – les Portalas – Roque des Bancs – Car park

Location: Apt, 222m in the Calavon Valley.

Starting point: Take the D 3 to Bonnieux, then onto the D 36 in the direction of Lourmarin. After nearly 2km turn right onto the narrow, asphalted forest road to the Massif des Cèdres. This is a toll road and ends after a very panoramic stretch at a car park (about 700m), 20km from Apt. From here further driving is prohibited.

Walking time: Car park – les Portalas: nearly 45 min; les Portalas – Well No 41: 45 min; Well – Roque des Bancs – Forestry road: 45 min; Forestry road – car park: 1 hr; total time: almost 3¼ hrs.

Ascent: About 100m.

Highest point: 713m on the forest road.

Grade: The first loop is an easy, mainly shady walk on well-marked paths and is also suitable for children. The second is also mainly an easy marked path, but there is a short section without a path where a degree of sure-footedness and a sense of direction are required.

Alternative: Both loops can be done independently of each other; the first requires almost 1½ hrs; the second 2 hrs. The ascent via the Roque des Bancs can be avoided, by following the cliff to its end, and then going north to the forest road (only slightly more time required, but there is no path as such).

Places of Interest: The village of Bonnieux is worth a visit in view of its picturesque little lanes, full of nooks and crannies, its panoramic position on the side of the hill and its Romanesque church.

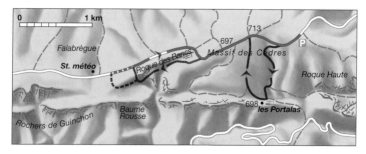

The first loop of the walk follows the nature trail through the most beautiful part of the cedar forest; the second takes in the wild escarpment of the Roque des Bancs. Both sections offer views into the distance and are easy to walk.

From the **car park**, after a few metres of the closed forest road, take the left turn to the »Sentier botanique«. Here there is a large notice board for the botanical trail, the various parts of which are followed on this walk. The rather stony path leads past a few cedars and then the vegetation becomes thinner

View into the distance from the viewpoint at les Portalas in the Petit Luberon.

and bushes dominate. At first it goes slightly downhill with views into the Durance Valley, then there is a steep and rather rocky uphill section, exposed to the sun, onto the ridge as far as the splendid viewpoint of **les Portalas** (698m), high over the Durance Valley (almost 45 min). Here the view ranges from the Alpes-de-Haute-Provence over the mountain of Ste-Victoire as far as the Alpilles; in clear weather even the Mediterranean can be seen on the horizon. The route now continues in a northerly direction almost without ascent into the most beautiful part of the cedar forest. Some of the trees are gigantic and provide pleasant shade. After a further good 30 minutes the tarmac road is reached again, along which (left) after just 15 minutes gently downhill well No 41 is reached. Here take a blue-marked path to the left through open scrub at a point where the road has a right-hand bend. At the first branch follow the path to the right and dropping down slightly arrive at the 25 m high rock barrier of the **Roque des Bancs**. The walk now goes along the bottom of the light-coloured limestone cliffs as far as an old sheepfold. Here, do not take the downhill path, but rather continue without a path to the north via the escarpment onto the plateau, where by continuing to walk in the same direction, the tarmac road is reached (45 min). This leads to the right with a scarcely perceptible rise back to the well. During this circuit there are repeated beautiful views to the north and south from the Luberon ridge. From the well there is an easy walk back to the **car park** over the high-level road (1 hr).

23 Mourre Nègre, 1125m

The »normal route« to the highest summit of the Luberon

Auribeau – Coteau de Bruny – Mourre Nègre and back

Location: Apt, 222m in the Calavon Valley.
Starting point: Take the narrow D 48 from Apt via the old village of Saignon to reach a car park in Auribeau at the turn off to the Route Forestière (about 600m), 8km from Apt. It is possible to continue for another kilometre along the gravelled forestry road to a second car park; this is however only to be recommended early in the morning or outside the walking season, as the number of parking spaces is very limited.
Walking time: Car park – Col d'Auribeau (P. 953m) 1½ hrs; Col – Summit: 45 min; Descent: almost 1¾ hrs; total time: just under 4 hrs.
Ascent: About 525m.
Highest point: Mourre Nègre, 1125m.
Grade: The path does not present any real

problems; although it is only marked in the upper section there are no navigation difficulties.
Alternative: If you continue from the summit along the GR in an easterly direction it is possible to descend leftwards to Castellet along a narrow yellow-marked path (sure-footedness required). After Castellet continue in a northerly direction along a minor road and then along a yellow-marked track back to the starting point (good 100 metres of ascent and almost an hour extra).
Places of Interest: Apt, which is known for its candied fruit, has an old cathedral (12th – 14th cent), a small archaeological museum and an Information Centre about the Luberon Nature Reserve.

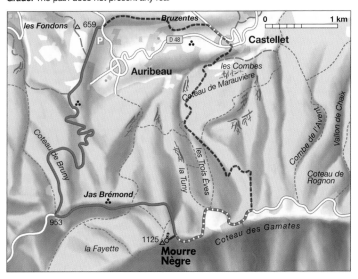

The lengthy ridge of the Grand Luberon on Mourre Nègre.

This walk is the easiest way of ascending the highest mountain of the Luberon via its wooded north side. The Mourre Nègre is a popular and much-visited summit on summer weekends and in clear weather offers a grandiose panorama from the Alps to the Mediterranean.

From the large **car park** follow the gravelled forestry road, which gently ascends to the second car park (15 min). From here onwards driving is prohibited in order to protect the Nature Reserve. Continue steadily uphill along the forestry road through an open forest, mainly consisting of downy oaks. In clear weather there are repeated views into the valley basin of Apt and towards Mont Ventoux. It is only in the freshness of the early morning that this part of the walk is pleasantly cool; otherwise the undertaking turns into a hot and sweaty undertaking. The road continues with broad, sweeping bends until a long section cuts across the slopes of the **Coteau de Bruny** and then leads at a height of 953m to a well at the **Col of Auribeau** (1¼ hrs) the point from where the Durance Valley can be reached. Here take the small, stony road to the left, which also has the red-white GR waymarkings on it. The road leads gently upwards first on the Durance Valley side and then on the Calavon side. On several occasions the path presents views down into the depths of both valleys and repeatedly cuts across small woods consisting of downy oaks, beech and pines, which alternate with garrigue vegetation. Keep to the right at a second well and after about 100m on a steep narrow road the flat crest of the **Mourre Nègre** is reached (about 45 min from the Col). The feeling of summit elation is unfortunately not, however, permitted to the walker, as a fenced off radio mast occupies the highest point.

24 Around the Abbey of St-Roman

A unique cliff church and wide views over the lower Rhone Valley

Car park – Abbey – St-Roman – Water Tower – Car park

Location: Tarascon, 9m.
Starting point: From Tarascon cross the Rhone to Beaucaire, which is left via the D 999 to the west. After 5km at a roundabout, where the road meets a ring road, go right along the parish road to St-Roman. After about 2km stop at the car park to the left on the roadside, 7km from Tarascon.
Walking time: Car park – Abbey – St-Roman: 1 hr; St-Roman – Water tower – car park: 1¼ hrs; total time: 2¼ hrs.
Ascent: About 120m.
Highest point: Abbey of St-Roman, 130m.
Grade: Well marked on the first section, the second section is unmarked and requires a certain sense of direction. Except for a short section on asphalt, it is mainly stony gravelled tracks, which, with the exception of the ascent to the water tower, are not particularly strenuous.
Places of Interest: In Beaucaire it is worth visiting the 13th century castle ruins, which offer a panoramic view of the Rhone Valley from the castle precincts. Also the beautiful town hall from the 17th century is worth visiting.

The peacefulness of the landscape reflected in the unique situation of the underground cliff abbey of St-Roman, and the beautiful views of the Rhone, lend this walk its particular charm.

From the **car park** follow the red-white waymarked GR 6 in a northerly direction (sign: »Abbaye«). The gravelled road leads slightly uphill through shady scrub and after a second car park becomes a paved track. After 20 minutes there is a spur path to the right, which leads to the abbey. The short detour requires about 10 minutes there and back (without visiting). The **abbey** was hewn out of the cliffs in the 12th – 13th century, abandoned in the 16th century and then built into a fortress, and destroyed about 1850. From the terrace there is a wonderful panoramic view. Visiting the unique building (along narrow paths) requires some care. With luck a green lizard may be seen. Back again at the above-mentioned turning-off, follow the GR to the

Graves in the ruins of the Abbey of St-Roman with the Rhone in the background.

right, almost level, through a jungle-like growths of Aleppo pines, holm oaks, rock roses and garrigue vegetation until open land is reached. Pay attention to markings and the path eventually leads not too-steeply down to the valley to an aqueduct at the beginning of the town of **St-Roman** (30 min). Go under the former water channel and carry straight on along the road through St-Roman (the GR branches off to the left en route) as far as a canal at the end of the town (good 10 min). Immediately before the bridge take the meadow path on the right and go down the canal to a tarmac road. Go right and then immediately left at a transformer station. Carry on along an abandoned railway embankment for some distance to the canal. Before a bridge which connects to a tunnel, climb down the bank to the right to the edge of a rubbish tip (just under 25 min). Here stay on the left edge from where a water tower can be seen above one to the left. Keep an eye on the water tower and at the upper end of the rubbish tip follow a narrow, rocky, unmarked path steeply up the left-hand slope to the **water tower** (10 min). Here follow a path on the right, which is also rocky and without markings, and which leads along the slope to an aqueduct. Here turn off left onto a track, which first to the south, then in a slight right-hand curve, leads on the level around the hill of the abbey. Stay on the main path, ignoring turnings which go up or down the hill. At the second car park the approach path is met again and the red and white markings are followed back to the starting point (30 min).

25 St-Rémy and Lac Peirou

An Alpine path and charming remains from Roman times

Lac Peirou – rock tunnel – Glanum – St-Rémy – Lac Peirou

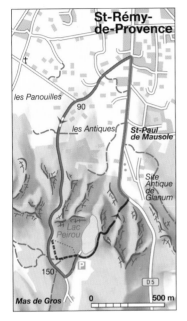

Location: St-Rémy-de-Provence (60m).

Starting point: From the town centre take the D 5 in the direction of les Baux and after almost a kilometre follow the »Barrage« sign on the right. A narrow tarmac road leads towards the mountain to the reservoir and car park (about 130m), 3km from the town centre.

Walking time: Lac Peirou – rock tunnel – D 5 at Glanum: 45 min; Glanum – St-Rémy – Lac Peirou: 1 hr; total time: 1¾ hrs.

Ascent: About 150m.

Highest point: Upper end of the rock tunnel, almost 200m.

Grade: Well-marked paths and marked roads with no navigation difficulties; nevertheless, the ascent from the lake requires sure-footedness and a head for heights, as craggy ground and a rock tunnel with iron rungs have to be overcome.

Places of Interest: In addition to the monuments described in the text below, a visit to the old town of St-Rémy with its narrow alleys, shady squares with fountains and plane trees, the Hôtel Estrine with the Van Gogh Centre and the Ancient History museum in the Hôtel de Sade is worthwhile.

The path leads past ancient and mediaeval monuments, which are very much worth seeing, crosses through an atmospheric forest, skirts a picturesque lake and finally, from the point of view of the ground and the scenery, takes on an alpine character.

From the car park go along the red and white marked GR 6 for a few metres to the **Peirou Reservoir** (about 130m), which was constructed in 1891 as a drinking water reservoir. If the small dam wall and the southern vegetation are ignored, the comparison with a mountain lake does not seem out of place. Follow the waymarkings, which lead through an open coniferous forest for a section on the right bank of the lake; then without warning the path leads steeply uphill. The landscape now shows its most beautiful side: the blue-green of the water, the green of the trees, the blueness of the sky

An almost alpine landscape at Lac Peirou near St-Rémy-de-Provence.

and the grey-white limestone crags offer an atmospheric contrast. The narrow path leads up over craggy ground and smooth rocks, thus necessitating the use of the hands. Finally there is a narrow rope-protected section under a rock wall. This ends at a rock tunnel, through which the route continues steeply diagonally upwards with the help of iron rungs, like in a chimney. After the tunnel the well-marked path again leads steeply downwards, only briefly interrupted by a level section. Scrub and rocky terrain eventually lead down into the valley, where the D 5 is met (45 min). Follow this to the left (GR markings). From the road there are some worthwhile detours. First stop is at the excavations of the Gallic-roman settlement of **Glanum** (signposted), which is worth a visit. Shortly after on the left of the road is the municipal Roman single-arched triumphal arch and the mausoleum of Julier, an empty grave for the nephew of Augustus, from whose time both monuments derive. The next stop is on the right in a side road: the monastery of St-Paul-de-Mausole, whose church and cloister with decorated stone chapter, are from Roman times. After a total of nearly a kilometre (15 min) on the D 5, a narrow tarred road leads off left back to the lake (signpost »barrage«). It first leads along on the flat past the last houses of **St-Rémy** and then goes gently uphill. At a nameless col (about 150m) it is possible to either take the minor road or a short cut on the left through the wood, which leads a short way downhill and then left along the GR 6 back to the **car park** (about 45 min).

26 The panorama from la Caume, 389m

The highest point of the Alpilles with plenty of forest and panoramic views

Col on the D 5 – Plateau de la Caume – Rocher des Deux Trous – D 5

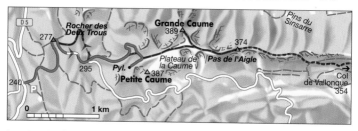

Location: St-Rémy-de-Provence, 60m.

Starting point: From St-Rémy take the wide D 5 to the south and after 5km of winding road reach a car park on the left at a nameless col on the ridge of the Alpilles (240m).

Walking time: Car park – la Caume – P. 374: 1½ hrs; P. 374 – Rocher des Deux Trous – car park: 1¾ hrs; total time: 3¼ hrs.

Ascent: About 150m.

Highest point: Grande Caume, 389m.

Grade: Generally easy walking along paths which are not always marked, but which nevertheless hardly present any navigation problems. It is only in the descent from the Rocher des Deux Trous and in the detour to Point 374m that sure-footedness is a requirement.

Alternative: Whoever wishes to can continue the ridge walk in an easterly direction as far they want before the GR after the Col de Vallonque (354 m) leads to the valley. The path is narrow and leads up and down over craggy ground at several points so that sure-footedness is absolutely necessary.

Places of Interest: Les Baux, 5km to the south on a 200m high crag is unfortunately often overrun with tourists. Its upper town has been a ruin since the destruction by Richelieu (1691). In the lower town some houses and a church have been restored. In particular the splendid situation and the views make it worth a visit.

On this very varied walk it feels at first as if one is in a botanical garden, then the deeply-fissured crags look like a film set from a Karl-May film, and at the end one is rewarded with a fantastic view.

From the **car park** go gently upwards in an easterly direction through thick, green vegetation along the closed tarmac road (sign »La Caume«). Pines, larches, juniper, and in spring, many flowering rock roses, bring the landscape to life. After the Vallon de St-Clerg the vegetation becomes more open. Shortly after, the road joins the GR 6. The minor road now changes over to the north side of the ridge, where there are fine views of bizarre rock formations, and climbs up more steeply in long drawn out bends in the direction of the summit of the **Petite Caume** (387m). (The GR goes straight up the slope.) When the road ends at a transmitter, go a few paces towards

»The crag with two holes« at la Caume – a whim of nature.

the south edge of the plateau with splendid views (1 hr). Back again at the transmitter take the red and white marked GR 6 on the right. It leads almost on the flat over the plateau with its many views. To go to the not very prominent summit of the **Grande Caume** (389m) turn off to the left and follow the path which goes past the built up summit a short distance to the north to the edge of the cliffs (15 min). Back again on the GR, follow this for a section to the east. Soon the plateau becomes a narrow ridge. Go down a short, rocky gully and then steeply up again to **Point 374m** (15 min), the turning point of the walk. The panoramic view reaches from the Montagne Ste-Victoire (east) past Mont Ventoux (north) to the Carmague (south). Now go back on the same path to the Petite Caume (30 min), where on reaching the minor road (here right) go immediately left following the steep direct descent of the GR, then left again to continue on the road (ignoring where the GR forks off). After a further 30 minutes follow the yellow waymarkings on the right, which are hardly visible through the scrub, up to the prominent **Rocher des Deux Trous**. Here take the unmarked path on the left steeply upwards to a crest with good views, and then go right, down the ridge, with good views to the road. There turn off right and arrive back at the **car park** either on the road or just to the side of it (45 min).

27 Étang de Berre

A quiet, undisturbed spot at an industrialised lake of brackish water

Étang de Berre – la Suzanne – le Bouquet – Étang de Berre

Location: Aix-en-Provence 177m.
Starting point: Leave Aix on the D 10 to the west and after about 25km go south (left) on the D 21 via St-Estève to the D 54. Turn right there and drive to the end of the road at the Étang de Berre (0m), where there are sufficient places to park, 35km of tarmac roads from Aix.

Walking time: Étang de Berre – la Suzanne: 40 min; la Suzanne – le Bouquet: 45 min; le Bouquet – Étang de Berre: 20 min; total time: 1¾ hrs.
Ascent: None.
Grade: Walking on roads (at times asphalted) and tracks, which are not marked, and therefore require some navigation ability, but otherwise no difficulties. On account of wetness in some sections of the walk, good boots or even Wellingtons are recommended.
Alternative: From le Bouquet it is possible to go for another kilometre along the bank of the Étang towards the north (about 15 min), in parts rather wet, but very peaceful and with good views of the lake, returning by the same path.
Places of Interest: To the north is the viewpoint of Lançon with a view of the Étang de Berre and the surrounding hills and in St-Chamas there is a Roman bridge (Pont Flavien) with a triumphal arch over the Touloubre (1st cent).

The walk includes still-peaceful corners with much undisturbed landscape at the Étang de Berre, which in its southern parts presents a sorry picture, with its many industrial developments.

From the side of the Étang enjoy the view of the still largely natural northern part of the lake and the adjacent hills – the quiet lapping of the waves and the calls of the gulls, almost allow the observer to forget the sins against the environment committed by industry in the southern part. From the **car park** go along the D 54 approach road, at first through high reeds towards the east. The narrow tarmac road is very little used; it goes through fields and allows a wide view as far as the chain of hills in the north, but also to the numerous industrial sites in the south. Keep following the D 54 straight on until the hamlet of **la Suzanne** where the road takes a 90° turn to the right (40 min). Here take the minor road that turns off left and leads to the west past la Suzanne. About 350m further on, the farm of l'Auranne is reached where the tarmac ends. Leave the farm on the left, and a few metres after the end of the tarmac you will come to a vineyard. Here keep left and go between the vineyard (right) and the farm (left) as far as a track, which is followed straight on to the D 54A. Cross over the road and continue the walk to the west on the other side. After a few fields the landscape becomes more isolated and more unspoilt. The track changes its direction slightly towards the north-west; ignore a turning off to the south (left). However, go to the west (i.e. turn left) at the next fork to reach the deserted farmhouse of **le Bouquet** (45 min), at a beautiful spot on the Étang de Berre, where the peace and the expanse of the water can be enjoyed. Here take the path in a southerly direction (left), which goes along close to the side of the lake through a landscape of reeds and marsh with very wet sections and which ends at the D 54. Here go to the right back to the **car park** in a few minutes (15 min).

Tranquil landscape of the Étang de Berre at le Bouquet.

28 The Bimont and Zola Lakes

Two lakes, a gorge and the rock mass of Ste-Victoire

Lac du Bimont – le Barrage – Lac Zola – les Infernets – Lac du Bimont

Location: Aix-en-Provence, 177m.

Starting point: From Aix drive along the D 10 in an easterly direction and turn right in St-Marc-Jaumegarde onto the D 101 to reach the car park at Lac du Bimont (353m), 10km from Aix.

Walking time: Lac du Bimont – le Barrage – Lac Zola: good 1¼ hrs; Lac Zola – les Infernets – Lac du Bimont: almost 1¼ hrs; total time: 2½ hrs.

Ascent: About 140m.

Highest point: 370m at le Barrage.

Grade: Good, well-marked paths that present no difficulties.

Advice: From 1st July to the second Sunday in September the path is closed because of the danger of forest fires and the railings at the far end of the dam wall of Bimont are locked: there are drastic penalties for any breach of the regulations! To be on the safe side in case of any changes, it is best to check on current regulations.

Places of Interest: From the point of view of the landscape a drive around the mountain of Ste-Victoire is very beautiful; the castle of Vauvenargues, where Picasso lived and is buried, cannot be visited.

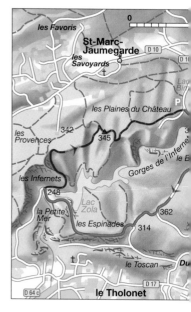

The two artificial lakes of Zola and Bimont with their clear water brighten up the sombre landscape around the wild, furrowed, infernal-gorge and the rugged Massif de Ste-Victoire, a favourite motif of the painter Cézanne.

From the car park the dam wall of the **Lac du Bimont** is reached in a few minutes by following the road to the east. (From 1.3 to 31.10 the gate to the dam is open from 7 – 22 hrs, otherwise from 9- 18 hrs.) From the crest there are splendid views into the depths of the infernal gorge (Gorges de l'Infernet) and towards the west flank of Ste-Victoire, which is mirrored in the clear waters of the lake. Shortly afterwards take the wide red-marked forestry track on the right, passing a barrier with an information board from the forestry authorities. This leads gently uphill through the woods to a fork on the heights of **le Barrage** (20 min; 370m). Keep to the right (further red markings) and walk almost on the flat through a pine forest which has been marked by the great fire in 1989, along a broad ridge high above the gorge, to another fork (P. 362m). Again take the right-hand path (the left leads to the Refuge Cézanne) and descend 50 metres in height along the path, which is now marked with green as well as red, to the next fork (P. 314m; 30 min). Here leave the red markings and instead follow the green ones, which lead gently upwards along the top of the ridge above the steep drop to the Doudon Valley. The path then turns to the north and drops down more steeply to the fjord-like **Lac Zola**. Cross the dam wall with fine views across the lake (248m; 30 min), which was built by the father of the writer, Emile Zola. Shortly after take the yellow-marked path on the right, which with an increased gradient leads up out of the **Gorges de l'Infernet**. On the plateau keep to the yellow markings again (right) and follow the path, which winds along on the edge of the plateau without any great change in height. Fine views of the Montagne Ste-Victoire and into the depths of the impressive Gorges de l'Infernet complete a varied circuit back to the car park at the **Lac du Bimont** (almost 1¼ hrs).

Sunflower field above the Gorges de l'Infernet.

29 Croix de Provence, 946m

Ascent of the Mountain of Cézanne via the classic route

Les Cabassols – Croix de Provence and back

Location: Aix-en-Provence, 177m.

Starting point: Leave Aix on the D 10 to the east and after 12km park at the houses of les Cabassols, either at the signposted car park or at one of the few parking spots at the beginning of the path. (369m).

Walking time: Les Cabassols – Croix de Provence: good 2 hrs; way back: just under 1¾ hrs; total time: 3¾ hrs.

Ascent: About 590m.

Grade: Well marked, but rocky mountain track that requires sure-footedness and a bit of a head for heights: strenuous if hot. There is no water en route!

Advice: On account of the danger of forest fires the path may not be left in the period from July 1st to the 2nd Saturday in Septem-

ber (use of other paths forbidden); no walking is allowed in periods of strong wind during this time. For your own safety do observe any notices (high penalties!).

Alternative: When permitted it is worthwhile to make a detour to the east along the panoramic ridge to the Col de Subéroque, the start of a difficult descent to the north (good 1¾ hrs, slightly up and down).

Places of Interest: Aix-en-Provence: the one-time capital city has an old quarter with beautiful houses and the plane tree lined Cours Mirabeau. Especially worth seeing are the Musée Granet (archaeology and paintings, among others from Cézanne) and the Cathedral of St-Saveur (12th – 16th cent).

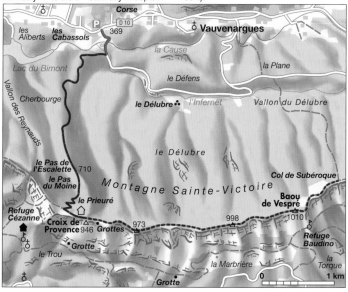

La Croix de Provence: Cézanne's favourite motif in the evening sun.

This walk with fine views leads into the Massif de Ste-Victoire, so often painted by Cézanne, which arises from the plain like a mighty block with an off-putting south side and a tame north one.

From the **car park** go for a few metres along the road in the direction of Vauvenargues, until the red and white marked GR 9 forks off (parking here, too). The path, called the Chemin des Venturiers, first goes slightly downhill in the shade, crosses two streams (Cause and Infernet) and soon after goes up through an open forest with pines, bushes and rock roses. In this section the forest track is very steep and rocky (also short concreted sections). At times there are fine views back into the valley, to Lac du Bimont and onto the mountains in the north (Luberon and Mt. Ventoux). At about 700m in height leave the forest and gain a mountain track, which is exposed to the sun. Slowly gain in height with the priory in view. After just under 2 hours the **Prieuré Notre-Dame** (900m) is reached. From the terrace of the 17th century building, which was lived in until 1879, perched on the hill like an eyrie, there is a wonderful view to the south.

To the back of the priory continue to the left past the cloister and go up through rocky terrain where it is necessary to scramble at one point, taking care on the polished, blank rock, to arrive at the **Croix de Provence** (946m; 10 min). In clear weather the panoramic view from here is fantastic. It extends from Mont Ventoux and Luberon in the north, to the Alpilles in the west, from Étoile and Ste-Baume in the south to the High Provence in the east. (Beware of the steep drop on the south side!)

30 Digue à la Mer and Étang de Vaccarès

In the nature reserve on the edge of the large salt lake

Phare de la Gacholle – Pont de Rousty – Saintes-Maries-de-la-Mer and back

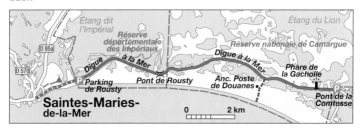

Location: Salin-de-Giraud, 0m.

Starting point: From Salin, first drive along the D 36 to the north and then onto the narrow D 36 C to the west. After St-Bertrand turn left at le Paradis in the direction of the Phare de la Gacholle and right again at a pumping station. The last 4km lead over a fairly worn out nature road which may not be driven along when there is a high tide and strong winds as it floods. At Pont de la Comtesse (0m) at the beginning of the nature reserve a car park is reached, 17km from Salin-de-Giraud.

Walking time: Pont de la Comtesse – Pont de Rousty: 2 hrs; Pont de Rousty – Parking in Rousty: 1 hr; Return route: 3 hrs; total time: 6 hrs (without detours).

Ascent: none.

Grade: Walking without problems on good

paths, but some fitness required due to the length of the walk.

Advice: To watch birds one is strongly recommended to take binoculars: the earlier the start, the better the opportunity for bird watching. From April to November mosquitoes can be a real nuisance, so take precautions. Also avoid starting when the mistral is strong or in bad weather. Unfortunately there are professional car thieves in the Camargue, so it is important to leave the car absolutely empty.

Places of Interest: At Pont de Gau there is the Ginès Information Centre for the Camargue Regional Nature Park and a bird park with many species. A little to the west Aigues-Mortes has a fully-preserved, imposing town wall from the 13th century.

A path without difficulties allows one to get to know the typical natural beauties of the Carmague: the sea, saltwater lakes, birds, dunes, etcetera. From the »**Phare de la Gacholle**« car park in front of the Pont de la Comtesse go straight on over the bridge and enter the Camargue National Reserve. It is absolutely essential to follow the regulations in the protected area and not to leave the permitted paths (this includes not going into the dunes). Keep walking on the flat towards the west for a good kilometre along the **Digue à la Mer**, a 19th century dyke, to reach the Gacholle lighthouse after a good kilometre. The continuation of the walk follows the dyke. The

Sunset over the Étang dit l'Impérial at Saintes-Maries-de-la-Mer.

route goes past salt lakes (étangs), lagoons, marshy land and the many dispersed islands of the **Étang de Vaccarès** – a wild, beautiful and still unspoilt landscape. About 2km past the Phare de la Gacholle it is possible to go left along the old smuggler path via what was a customs post and along a broad sandy beach directly to the sea (about 2km there and back) – a fine alternative for all those for whom the walk to Saintes-Maries is too long (altogether a good 2¼ hrs). However, to continue the suggested walk, go on along the Digue à la Mer. In the morning it is possible to see many birds here, especially the various seagulls, flamingos, spectacled warblers, terns, stilts and ducks. After 2 hours cross the **Pont de Rousty** and go from the Camargue National Reserve into the Réserve départementale des Impériaux. To the left there is now mainly sand and dunes, to the right the part of the Étang de Vaccarès known as the Étang dit l'Impérial. After a further hour the Parking de Rousty is reached at the »Chenal de Vitesse« canal, the end of the dyke and the beginning of the road to **Saintes-Maries-de-la-Mer**. For those for whom the walk is not too long, this detour can be undertaken on foot (good hour there and back along a rather less beautiful route). Unfortunately the town is overrun with tourists, particularly in the period of the gipsy pilgrimage (24 –25th May and on the first Sunday after the 22nd October). The town itself has a Romanesque church with a reliquary, pleasant lanes in the old town and a lot of beach. The way back from the Parking de Rousty follows the same route, unless one has a second car parked there.

31 Étang de Galabert and Étang du Fangassier

A small circuit in typical Carmague landscape

Pumping station – Pont de la Comtesse – Martelières du Fangassier – Pumping station

Location: Salin-de-Giraud, 0m.
Starting point: From Salin follow the same route as for the previous walk, but parking instead on the side of the road at the pumping station (0m), 1.5km from the

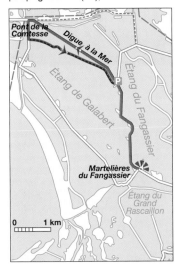

beginning of the Nature Trail which is closed when flooded, 15km from Salin.
Walking time: Pumping station – Pont de la Comtesse: 45 min; Pont de la Comtesse – Martelières du Fangassier: 1¾ hrs; Martelières du Fangassier – Pumping station: 45 min; total time: 3¼ hrs.
Ascent: None.
Grade: Easy walking on unmarked nature trails; no navigation problems.
Advice: Do not forget your binoculars for birdwatching; for this purpose you should get started as early as possible. Make sure you leave your car empty as professional thieves operate here. Take precautions against mosquitoes and do not set out in strong winds or rain.
Places of Interest: In la Capellière there is an interesting Information Centre for the Camargue Reserve and the Étang de Vaccarès, with a nature trail, and bird hides. The museum in Mas du Pont de Rousty provides excellent information on the history of the Camargue. A further worthwhile excursion is to the impressive Romanesque church of St-Gilles (portal, crypt) with its famous winding staircase.

The walk leads along dykes through the typical landscape of the southern Camargue, with its salt-water lakes, and from where many birds, in particular flamingos, can be seen from close up. The walk goes through a charming landscape, which is still not overfilled with tourists.
From the **pumping station** follow the road (in a north-westerly direction) to the Phare de la Gacholle (see previous walk). It leads along a dyke, on which juniper-like bushes and camomiles grow, between two murky saltwater lakes (étangs). The view sweeps across the apparently endless water landscape. Along the way there are plenty of opportunities to watch birds, especially flamingos, spectacled warblers and gulls. Continue along the worn out

nature road towards the lighthouse (Phare de la Gacholle), to reach the **Pont de la Comtesse**, the border of the Nature Reserve of the Étang de Vaccarès (45 min). Immediately before the bridge and the reserve turn off left onto a dyke, and nearly 500 metres further on turn left again onto a dyke which runs roughly parallel to the approach route. Go along past maritime grasses and low shrubs to reach another linking dyke near the pumping station (1 hr). The colourful bee-eaters can also frequently be seen here. To the left it is only a few paces back to the start of the walk, but instead of returning take a detour to the right (in a southerly direction) along the dyke between the two Étangs. The worn out nature track leads in 45 minutes to a viewpoint. (Keep left where the road is joined by another road from the right). The viewpoint – **Martelières du Fangassier** has a view of the three salt-water lakes: the Étang de Galabert, Étang du Fangassier and the Étang du Grand Rascaillon. Once again the impressive landscape with its many birds (including shell-duck and avocets) can be enjoyed to the full. On the small island of Îlot du Fangassier is found the only breeding colony of lesser flamingos in Europe. The return route, direct to the pumping station takes the same path (45 min).

Yellow irises and wild roses line a stream at la Capellière.

32 Pilon du Roi

A rock pillar like a giant menhir

Mimet car park – Col Ste-Anne – Pilon du Roi – Car park

Location: Gémenos, 150m.
Starting point: Leave Gémenos on the N 396 and then take the N 96 to the north via Roquevaire to la Destrousse. Here take the D 7 via Peypin, Cadolive and St-Savournin to the west until the D 8 D to Mimet turns off. 3.5km past Mimet in the direction of Col Ste-Anne park in front of a barrier (about 540m), 24km from Gémenos.
Walking time: Car park – Pilon du Roi: 1 hr; Pillon du Roi – Car park: 1¼ hrs; total time: 2 ¼ hrs.
Ascent: About 140m.
Highest point: About 680m on the ridge at a signal station.

Grade: Although there are not always waymarks, navigation is not a problem, nor is the walking difficult. On the Pilon du Roi some sure-footedness is useful.
Advice: On account of the terrible forest fires in 1997 in the Étoile Mountains, you can expect the area to be closed from the beginning of July until the beginning of September. Check before setting out.
Places of Interest: The large city of Marseille with its numerous museums, the old la Major cathedral, the Basilica of St-Victor, the harbour, the J.F.Kennedy panoramic coastal road and the Château d'If on an island, is always worth a visit.

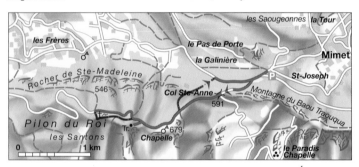

This panoramic circuit in the western part of the Chaîne de l'Étoile leads along an easy path to the Pilon du Roi, a gigantic rock pillar with difficult climbing walls where birds of prey also nest.

Go past the barrier behind the **car park** and carry on along the tarmac road (not the footpath to the right). This ascends gently through open scrub towards the **Col Ste-Anne** (591m). Immediately beyond the top of the pass take the blocked-off, unmarked gravel road, which runs evenly and with excellent views along the south side of the ridge. At a further col, switch over to the other side of the mountain ridge, staying on the gravelled road

Sign indicating the direction on a rock below the Pilon du Roi.

(10 metres of tarmac) that now has blue waymarks. The path goes up gradually through open forest. At a junction, keep to the blue waymarked road (straight on). In front of a signal station it is possible to go a few paces to the left to the ridge to get a view of the south slopes of the massif. A big forest fire blazed here in 1997. The road eventually ends after a final incline to the west around the signal station at a col (about 680m) with good views

The west flank of the limestone Chaîne de l'Étoile before the 1997 forest fire.

The path at the Col Ste-Anne with views to the north.

to the south of Marseille and the sea. To the west a narrow path with blue markings continues, and this runs along the south side of the ridge and allows fascinating glimpses of the steep north pillar of the **Pilon du Roi**. The path goes gently up and down directly along the base of the massive lump of rock (about 670m) the wall of which rises vertically above the path. A few metres later where the path splits (1 hr), take the right fork with green waymarks (sign on the rock »Sirmiane«). This crosses the ridge and leads down steeply on the north side through rocks and scrub. After 15 minutes it meets a forestry road, which is followed to the right, but without any waymarks. Proceeding gently uphill it affords gripping views of the north side of the Pilon. After a further 15 minutes the blue waymarked forestry road of the approach walk is reached, which is descended towards the left. Twenty minutes later the short, tarmac section mentioned above is reached. Here turn to the left along the white-red-white marked track (sign »parking«). This first leads almost on the level, with fine views to the north, around the furthest rock promontory of the massif, and then leads down gently to the valley through scrub. At the next junction it is possible to take either the left or the right fork. Both join up with a forestry road, which in very little time leads rightwards back to the **car park** (25 min).

33 Tête du Grand Puech, 778 m

The highest point of the massif – guaranteed view of the sea.

Car park at Mimet – Tête du Grand Puech – Col Ste-Anne – Car park

Location: Gémenos, 150m.
Starting point: Leave Gémenos on the N 396 and then take the N 96 to the north via Roquevaire to la Destrousse. Here take the D 7 via Peypin, Cadolive and St-Savournin to the west until the D 8 D to Mimet turns off. 3.5km past Mimet in the direction of Col Ste-Anne park in front of a barrier (about 540m), 24km from Gémenos.
Walking time: Car park – Grand Puech: 1¼ hrs; Grand Puech – Col Ste-Anne – Car park: 1½ hrs; total time: 2¾ hrs.
Ascent: About 240m.
Highest point: Tête du Grand Puech, 778m.
Grade: The leisurely ascent along a good forestry road presents no problems for navigation or fitness; the narrow path along the ridge with a steep and rocky descent does require sure-footedness.
Advice: See Walk 32.
Places of Interest: On account of its situation on top of a rock, Mimet has fine views, and there is a pleasant old town with a pedestrian area. To the south of the massif the stalactite caves of Loubière are worth visiting.

A Provencale relation of the white Alpine Poppy.

The ascent walk offers many fine views, but the panoramic views from the summit and the views from the ridge walk that follow are even better. Particularly impressive is the view of the Mediterranean to the south.

Immediately beyond the **car park** go past the barrier and shortly afterwards turn left at the signpost for the »Grand Puech« along a wide, almost flat forestry road that leads through open scrub. There are frequent fine views towards Mimet and the Montagne Ste-Victoire to the north. After about 20 minutes the gravelled road begins to steepen a

The broad chain of hills of the western Chaîne de l'Étoile from the ridge path.

bit and views become more extensive, spoilt only by an ugly bauxite factory at Gardanne. At the first bend (no signpost) take the wide forestry road on the right, which leads via a number of bends to the summit of the **Tête du Grand Puech** (778m; 1¼ hrs). Unfortunately the summit is somewhat disfigured by a military building, but it does offer fine views to the north. Now follow the blue markings, which begin here, and lead in a few minutes towards the southwest to the edge of the ridge; from here there is a splendid view over the Garlaban, Marseille and the Mediterranean. The marked path with fine views now leads first somewhat to the right, and then a bit to the left of the ridge, sometimes flat or slightly up or down hill. In spring the path is lined with many flowering rock roses. There are no difficult or exposed sections, but sure-footedness is a requirement. This charming section of the walk touches on the various elevations of the Montagne du Baou Traouqua, as this part of the Étoile Mountains is known. Towards the end there is a fascinating view into the depths of the almost vertical cliffs on the north side of the mountain (Beware of the drop!) At the end there is a steep and rocky descent with a craggy section, which requires some caution. At a high-tension mast a gravelled road is reached and shortly afterwards somewhat below the **Col Ste-Anne** (591m) a narrow tarmac road is joined, onto which you turn right. A few metres further on it crosses the pass and leads in a leisurely fashion down through scrub to the **car park** (1½ hrs).

34 Montagne de Regagnas

A peaceful ridge walk to an old hermitage

Pas de la Couelle – Col de Ribierre – St-Jean-du-Puy – Pas de la Couelle

Location: Gémenos, 150m.

Starting point: From Gémenos first drive to the north along the N 396 and N 96 as far as Pont-de-Joux, then westerly on the N 560 via Auriol to St-Zacharie. Here take the minor D 85 (later D 12), which is very winding, as far as the Pas de la Couelle (531m), 23km from Gémenos. There are parking places on the far side of the Pass where the road branches off to the hermitage.

Walking time: Pas de la Couelle – St-Jean-du-Puy: nearly 1¾ hrs; Return route: 50 min; total time: 2½ hrs (without detour).

Ascent: About 200m.

Highest point: St-Jean-du-Puy, 657m.

Grade: Mainly well-marked paths or minor roads: no navigation difficulties. For the ridge walk surefootedness is required, as the path is in parts overgrown with thorny scrub (long trousers recommended). Sweaty if it is hot.

Alternative: From the hermitage the walk can be extended as far as desired in the direction of Mont Aurélien. From the car park at the beginning of the road take the large DFCI forestry track on the right (north-east); this leads almost on the level at first close to the ridge, then gradually further away as far as a col (about 1 hr), a beautiful addition to the walk, with views to the south.

The walk to the hermitage of St-Jean-du-Puy offers splendid views of the Sainte-Victoire Massif and of the Ste-Baume Massif, and the return path leads through typical garrigue vegetation.

The path towards St-Jean-du-Puy, which is often overgrown with garrigue vegetation.

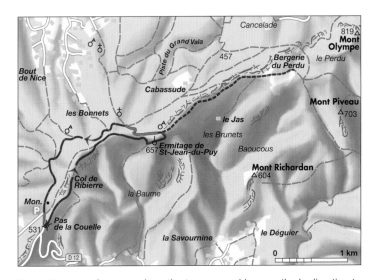

From the **car park,** go up along the tarmac road in a southerly direction to the **Pas de la Couelle** (531m; about 10 min). Here take the moderately steep, blue-marked path on the left, which runs along the sunny south side of the ridge and offers beautiful views of the Massif de la Ste-Baume. After an initial »summit«- the Montagne Ste-Victoire in the north also appears – a short section on the ridge goes downwards, and then the path leads steeply back uphill to a second rise and an equally short, steep section leads down to the Col de Ribierre. A gentler stretch then leads through a small forest followed by a more mountainous section. The blue-marked path is not exactly exposed but there are a couple craggy sections where you need to use your hands. Back on the ridge again the path soon leads back gently downhill. It now becomes fairly overgrown (prickly bushes, scrub and holly). After another dip stay on the marked path along the ridge, until it meets the GR 9, and then follow the red and white markings for a short section uphill to the **Ermitage de St-Jean-du-Puy** (657m; 1½ hrs). From the lookout tower at the hermitage there is a fantastic panoramic view: Chaîne de l'Étoile, Ste-Victoire, Ste-Baume. From here follow the GR 9, which leads slighty downhill through an open wood in the direction of Trets, which soon becomes a gravelled road. When the GR turns off to the right, keep going straight on along the minor road with orange waymarks, which, after two bends, is almost level. Fifty minutes of easy walking leads to the **car park.**

35 Col de Bertagne

In the little-known western part of the Massif de la Ste-Baume

Plan-d'Aups – Col de Bertagne – la Mine – Plan-d'Aups

Location: Gémenos, 150m.
Starting point: From Gémenos drive along the D 2, which is at first wide, but then narrow and windy, to the Col de l'Espigoulier and shortly after to a high plateau. Then take the D 80 to Plan-d'Aups, turning right there onto the Chemin de la Brasque for 300 m to a barrier and a car park (686m), 18km from Gémenos.
Walking time: Plan-d'Aups – Col de Bertagne: 45 min; Col de Bertagne – la Mine: 1¾ hrs; la Mine – Plan-d'Aups: 30 min; total time: 3 hrs.

Ascent: Nearly 200m.
Highest Point: Just under the Pics de Corbeaux (880m).
Grade: Some stretches of the walk are not marked, but with some care and a sense of direction it should not offer problems; the good paths and roads (some tarmac) present no technical difficulties.
Places of Interest: Shortly beyond Gémenos it is worth making a detour to the shady park of St-Pons with a picturesque spring and the remains of a Cistercian abbey (13th century).

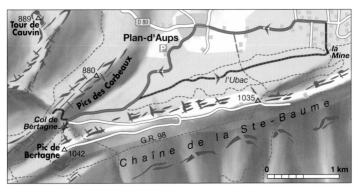

The walk offers many shady sections in a beautiful forest, but in the upper part there are views into the distance as well, where the massive rock shape of the Pic de Bertagne dominates the scenery.

From the **car park** take the tarmac but closed forestry road with the name »Col de Bertagne«, which leads gently in a southwesterly direction towards the mountain through a mixed forest, rich in species. Leave the road in a sharp left-hand bend along a path which goes straight on, and which after a few metres leads to the **Col de Bertagne** (45 min). From here there are impressive views of the steep walls of the Pic de Bertagne and beyond, over Gémenos, to the coast. Back on the tarmac road there is a further short

View from Col de Bertagne in the direction of Gémenos.

detour on the left. A gravelled road leads for a short distance uphill to a first saddle at the Pics des Corbeaux, which allows splendid views to the north as far as the Alps and continues in a 180° bend to a second saddle, from which a fine view of the rock mass of the Pic de Bertagne can be enjoyed (15 min, easy). Back again on the tarmac road, follow this downhill to the left. After about 20 minutes take the second forest track on the right with the sign »U 48 – L'Ubac« (white / olive green and white markings). This leads either on the level or slightly downhill through the Forest of Ste-Baume with its many types of trees. Keep right at the first fork, otherwise always straight on, watching out for markings. This leads to a second barrier at the end of the forest. Immediately afterwards take a gravelled track on the left, then a tarmac road to **la Mine**, which after a few minutes leads to a crossing (nearly an hr). Here go along the tarmac road with the name »Allée des Signes« which is lined by trees, and continues with no perceptible change in height to the D 80 to **Plan-d'Aups**. Follow the D 80 for a short way to the left and then turn left again into the next side road (Chemin de la Brasque) and after about 300 metres this leads back to the starting point (30 min).

36 St-Pilon, 994m and Joug de l'Aigle, 1118m

The classic walk in Ste-Baume through a unique forest

Hôtellerie – St-Pilon – Joug de l'Aigle – Hôtellerie

Location: Gémenos, 150m.

Starting point: As with the previous walk drive from Gémenos via the Col de l'Espigoulier to Plan-d'Aups and from there continue on the D 80 to the Hôtellerie de la Ste-Baume, where there are enough places to park on the side of the road on the right (669m), 22km from Gémenos.

Walking time: Hôtellerie – St-Pilon: 1¼ hrs; St-Pilon – Joug de l'Aigle: 45 min; Joug de l'Aigle – Hôtellerie: 1½ hrs; total time: 3½ hrs.

Ascent: About 500m.

Highest Point: Joug de l'Aigle, 1118m.

Grade: Well-marked paths without navigation difficulties, but which, nevertheless require sure-footedness: it is advisable not to go too near to the steep drop on the north ridge.

Alternative: From the summit of St-Pilon it is possible to go along the ridge to the west with only very little change in height as far as the beginning of the descent to the Col du Fauge (978m); very panoramic stretch, about 11km there and back. To the east to the highest point of the massif, Ste-Baume (1148m), it is 6km there and back, likewise with splendid views.

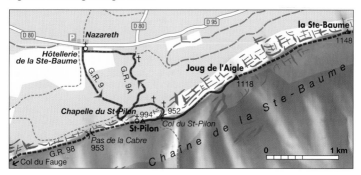

The path to St-Pilon leads through a thick mixed forest rich in species (especially beech, sycamore, lime and pines, but also yew), which is not typical of the Provence and reminds one more of northern latitudes. On the ridge a fantastic view opens out, which reaches from Mont Ventoux to the Mediterranean.

From the **car park** follow the red and white marked GR 9, which goes to the south from immediately east of the Hôtellerie. It leads over fields to the forest and there goes to the right at a fork in the path. The Massif of Ste-Baume with its steep rock faces appears very forbidding. To protect the unique forest you should stay on the path (some parts have had to be blocked off). The path leads steadily but not steeply uphill. At a chapel the GR 9 A joins it. Stay on

The small chapel on the summit of St-Pilon with a view to the Joug de l'Aigle.

the GR 9 (left and then immediately right), which now becomes steeper and rockier and leaves the forest. The wide path now runs along a rock wall, indeed it is partly cut into it, but it is not exposed. After this short intermezzo the **Col du St-Pilon** (952m) is reached, one of the only places in the massif where a crossing without problems is possible (a good hour). Here take the gently rising GR 98 and after 10 minutes reach the summit of **St-Pilon** (994m), which is crowned by a small church. From here there is an impressive panoramic view, which reaches from the sea, over Marseille as far as the Montagne Ste-Victoire (be careful as the ground drops away over 100m on the north side). Back again at the Col du St-Pilon, continue straight on, again on the GR 9. The red and white marked track goes along the south side of the sparsely vegetated ridge with fine views. Up to the next summit, the **Joug de l'Aigle** (1118m; 45 min) is not too steep, and a view awaits one similar to the superb view from St-Pilon. The descent to the Col du St-Pilon (30 min) and onwards to the fork at the chapel is the same path as for the ascent. Here turn off right and follow the similarly red and white marked waymarked GR 9 A. The wide road leads with a moderate downward incline through the forest into the valley. Here in front of a wooden fence a yellow-marked track forks off to the left (sign: »Hôtellerie«) which runs through the forest to join up with the GR 9, which is followed to the right over fields to the **car park** (1 hr from pass).

37 St-Probace and the Caramy Gorge

A secluded monastery and a delightful forested gorge

Moulin du Caramy – St-Probace – Gorges du Caramy – Moulin du Caramy

Location: St-Maximin-la-Ste-Baume, 303m.
Starting point: From St-Maximin drive along the N 7 to the southeast to Tourves. Go through the centre and at the eastern end go right at an acute angle into Av. Gaou, (narrow, numerous speed bumps) along next to a small stream almost parallel to the N 7. At the first possible place go under the Route National and follow the signpost to »Moulin du Caramy« left past the stadium. Just before the end of the asphalt a barrier is reached with a car park (275m), 11km from St-Maximin.

Walking time: Car park near Moulin du Caramy – St-Probace: nearly 45 min; St-Probace – Gorges du Caramy: 1¼ hrs; Gorges du Caramy – Moulin du Caramy: good 45 min; total time: 2¾ hrs.

Ascent: About 280m.

Highest point: 519m at St-Probace.

Grade: Mainly satisfactorily marked tracks, which do however, lead through some steep and craggy terrain; here sure-footedness is absolutely necessary.

Alternative: There is also the possibility at the spring to continue to the right to penetrate into the upper gorge of the Caramy (about 1.5km to its end); the path, however, can only be recommended to very experienced walkers.

Places of Interest: In St-Maximin-la-Ste-Baume there is the largest gothic church in the Provence (15th cent, old crypt).

The walk leads to the isolated, splendidly-situated chapel of St-Probace. Particularly charming is the path through the Gorge du Caramy, which on account of its lush vegetation has an almost jungle-like atmosphere.

From the **car park** continue along the blocked off approach road (a Roman bridge on the left-hand side) and stay for a short distance on the right bank

Steep cliffs and much forest dominate the scenery in the Gorges du Caramy.

of the Caramy. Turn right at the first possibility onto a path with old green waymarks, which leads up steeply in a northerly direction. The path leads through craggy, sparsely-vegetated terrain where it is occasionally necessary to make use of the hands. After an extremely strenuous ascent, the chapel of **St-Probace** - beautifully situated on the ridge – is reached (40 min). The place emanates peace, has a splendid view and in spring presents a fine display of flowers. The walk continues to the left, in a westerly direction along a path with blue waymarks. This begins along the ridge with fine views and then leads more steeply downhill in a southerly direction through open scrub. In a valley at a ruin the path meets a wide forestry track, which is followed down steeply to the left. In a right-hand bend go left into the forest along a narrow path, the blue waymarks for which only appear somewhat later. After a further downhill section take a track to the left with red markings before a large farmhouse (50 min). This first leads almost on the flat towards the east to the edge of the Plateau of St-Probace. The path then leads down the steep slope into the **Gorges du Caramy**, meeting up with the valley path at the la Figuière spring (25 min). The path, at first very narrow and rather overgrown, (occasional yellow or blue markings), leads down into the valley along the left bank of the picturesque stream with hardly any perceptible height change. The narrow gorge, hemmed in by steep cliffs and with almost jungle-like vegetation, is very impressive. At the derelict farmhouse of Bastide de Rimbert the track becomes wider and the valley opens out a little. Further downstream past a turning off to St-Probace (left) and to the Roman bridge (right) the starting point is reached again (50 min).

38 The three Calanques of Cassis

Fjord-like landscapes and the curse of tourism

Cassis – Calanque de Port-Pin – Calanque d'En-Vau and back

Location: Cassis, 4m.

Starting point: In Cassis it is best to park in the sign-posted car park »Parking de la Viguerie« somewhat above the harbour.

Walking time: Parking de la Viguerie – Calanque de Port-Pin: 45 min; Calanque de Port-Pin – Calanque d'En-Vau: 45 min; Calanque d'En Vau – Parking: 1½ hrs; total time: 3 hrs.

Ascent: About 420m.

Highest point: About 140m on the Plateau de Cadeïron.

Grade: The well-marked path has an mountainous quality in places and therefore demands sure-footedness and a head for heights. Scrambling on the shiny, polished cliffs requires particular care.

Refreshments: Numerous bars and restaurants in Cassis.

Alternative: A good map allows various other walks to be undertaken, e.g. there is an alternative approach route from the car park in Port Miou along the road to the la Fontasse youth hostel and from there along a forestry track to the south to the Plateau of Cadeiron to the GR 98 B (a good 30 min longer).

Advice: Do not leave any valuables in the car; high theft rate from cars.

Places of Interest: Cassis with its picturesque ambience of harbour, promenade and old town, is worth a visit.

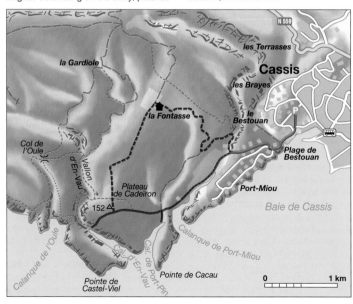

Southern Mediterranean charm in the Harbour of Cassis.

The walk to the Calanques leads through a spectacular coastal landscape with a fjord-like character, whose charm interacts with the colours of the sea, cliffs, sky and the open vegetation. Unfortunately all too many tourists have discovered this. In particular during the main holiday season (July/August) one should avoid Cassis, or set off for the walk early in the morning to experience the idyllic landscape at least half-undisturbed.

From the manned **carpark** »Viguerie« go leftwards along the street of the same name downhill in the direction of the harbour and keep following the signs to the Calanques. After a short hill the beautiful sandy beach of Bestouan is reached. Go up past magnificent houses over a second hill, and at the end of the road the car park of **Calanque de Port-Miou** is reached. On the north side of the »fjord« take the red and white waymarked GR 98 B on the left, which first goes along past a quarry (on the right). The path becomes narrower beyond a yacht harbour and the cliffs drop steeply into the sea. Cross a small ridge over extremely polished rocks, which demand caution, and go down more steeply through open wood to the **Calanque de Port-Pin** (45 min), which, with its shady beach and rocky walls provides an even more intensely beautiful landscape. Now the path winds up steeply over a slightly

The Yacht Harbour in the Calanque of Port-Miou.

vegetated slope to the **Plateau de Cadeïron** (about 140m), where it meets a forestry track. Keep following the waymarked GR, crossing the rise towards the west and then afterwards descending along a narrow, very steep path in zigzags over rough rocky steps and with some scrambling. At the end of the almost mountaineering descent, the most beautiful of the three bays, the Calanque d'En-Vau is reached (45 min). With its limestone white walls, the light coloured pebbled beach and the calm, blue-green water, this would be perceived as a truly idyllic landscape, were it not for the number of other people. The return path to **Cassis** via the approach path also takes 1½ hrs.

A ship makes for the picturesque Calanque of Port-Pin.

39 Cap Canaille and Grande Tête, 394m

Visit to the highest sea cliffs in France

Bec de l'Aigle – Grande Tête – Cap Canaille – Pas de la Colle and back

Location: Cassis, 4m.

Starting point: From Cassis drive eastwards along the narrow, steep D 41 A in the direction of Cap Canaille – Route des Crêtes. At the Pas de la Colle the panoramic high road begins which ends at the Sémaphore du Bec de l'Aigle (328m), about 11km from Cassis.

Walking time: Bec de l'Aigle – Pas de la Colle: good 1½ hrs; Return route: nearly 2 hrs; total time: 3½ hrs.

Ascent: About 300m.

Highest Point: Grande Tête, 394m.

Grade: Mainly narrow, well-marked paths, which at times require sure-footedness and a head for heights, although not particularly exposed.

Advice: In times of forest fire danger and high winds the path is closed for the protection of the walker. Do not go too close to the edge of the vertical cliffs.

Places of Interest: From la Ciotat small excursions to Île Verte, the Calanque de Figuerolles with its bizarre rocks and the Parc Mugel, with its rich vegetation and beautiful view of the town, are recommended.

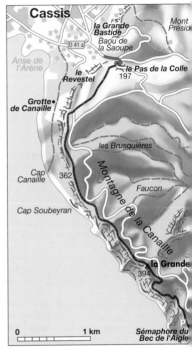

The walk with splendid views of the rugged coast between Marseille and la Ciotat leads to the highest sea cliffs in France and offers at the same time the proximity to the sea and the experience of a »proper« mountain walk.

From the car park at **Sémaphore** go a few paces to the left to the Orientation Table, which explains the details of the wide panoramic view from the cape: on one side the delightful coast between Bandol and la Ciotat, and on the other side the wild continuation of the coast via Cassis to the Montagne de Marseilleveyre. Then go in the opposite direction left of the approach road along the blue-waymarked ridge path (signpost) along the cliffs. At first the path, which is rocky, leads very slightly upwards through scrub vegetation (including rock roses, gorse, small pines). Then comes a steeper section to

The rocky path along the steep cliffs of the Grande Tête.

Grande Tête (394m), which offers a unique panoramic view. The barren landscape on the side of the path is dominated by ground-covering vegetation and bushes. The continuously blue-marked path is hardly exposed but it is rocky and in places the ground underfoot is somewhat crumbly, so that one should take care. The path leads from the Grande Tête equally steeply downhill, touches on the road and overcomes a small rounded hilltop. There are continuous wonderful views over the Bay of Cassis and of the coast to Marseille as well as of the mighty cliffs of the Montagne de la Canaille. Cross two further knolls thereby touching on the Route des Crêtes and finally go up to the **Cap Canaille** (362m), which is also a splendid viewpoint. After a further small rounded hilltop the path goes away from the ridge and leads down in a valley-like section until after a more pronounced dip the road is reached. From here it is only short distance down to the left to the **Pas de la Colle** (197m). A few paces further downhill in the direction of Cassis it is possible once again to observe the picturesque location of the place at the bay of the same name (good 1½ hrs). The way back is the same as the approach (nearly 2 hrs).

40 Sommet de l'Homme, 1637m

Isolated viewpoint in the Montagne de Lure

Refuge de Lure – P. 1700m – Sommet de l'Homme and back

Location: Forcalquier, 550m.
Starting point: From Forcalquier drive for a short distance along the N 100 to the west, then take the wide D 950 and D 13 to St-Étienne-les-Orgues. From there drive along the winding D 113 through beautiful forest to the Refuge de Lure (1590m) at the winter sports resort of the same name, 30km from Forcalquier.
Walking time: Ascent: good 1¾ hrs: Descent: nearly 1½ hrs; total time: 3¼ hrs.
Ascent: About 200m.
Highest point: P. 1700m.
Grade: Paths of very varying characteristics,

which are only marked in places. Sure-footedness is advisable for the ridge walk.
Alternative: If desired the panoramic ridge walk can be continued to the west. First go steeply down to Baisse de Malcort (1368m), then almost as steeply upwards to P. 1629m (about 2km).
Advice: See Walk 41.
Places of Interest: In Forcalquier the cemetery and the Franciscan monastery are worth a visit. An excursion to the Observatory of the Haute-Provence with its fine views is also to be recommended.

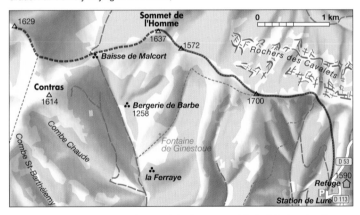

On the border between the Alps and the Provence this isolated walk offers an unspoilt experience of nature with wonderful views into the distance to the north and south.

From the car park a little above the **Refuge de Lure** cross the road and take the first forestry track on the left with the red and white GR 6 markings, which ascends almost imperceptibly. After a saddle (about 1650m; the GR forks off right) stay on the track which now has blue waymarks. This leads gently downhill (about 1600m) and uphill via barren pastureland and through open

View over the west ridge of the Montagne de Lure to the Sommet de l'Homme.

beech woods to a saddle in the ridge (about 1670m; 25min) – nice views to the north from here. While the forestry track leads to the left towards the valley, take the path to the right, which goes up a grassy slope on the south side of the ridge. Now follow the line of the ridge with its rises and in doing so enjoy fine views of the north flank, which although thickly wooded falls away steeply in places with the rocky inclines of the Rocher des Cavalets (take care where the ground drops away). The more gentle south side tends to be barren and rocky. The route, which is not too strenuous at first, leads up to a nameless summit (**P. 1700m**), the highest point on the walk. From here there is a similar panoramic view to that which is obtained later on the Sommet de l'Homme. Now there is a longer steeper downhill section to the lowest point of the whole walk (P. 1572m). This is followed by a less demanding ascent to the goal of the walk, the **Sommet de l'Homme** (1637m; almost 1½ hrs). The panorama from the summit is fantastic: as far as the Alps and Pre-Alps in the north, to Mont Ventoux in the west, to the Vaucluse Plateau and the Luberon in the south and to the Signal de Lure and the mountains of the Haute-Provence in the east. The way back is via the same route (almost 1½ hrs).

41 Signal de Lure, 1826m

Ridge walk with fine views to the highest point of the Montagne de Lure

Pas de la Graille – Signal de Lure – Refuge de Lure – Pas de la Graille

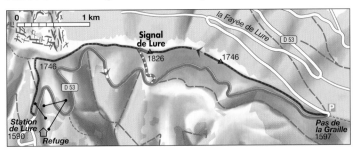

Location: Sisteron, 482m, in the Durance Valley.

Starting point: From Sisteron drive onto the D 53, then for a short while on the D 946 and then back onto the D 53 to the south, which soon winds its way up the hillside. After 30km of driving along the narrow tarmac road, park at the Pas de la Graille (1597m).

Walking time: Pas de la Graille – Signal de Lure: 1 hr; Signal de Lure – Refuge de Lure: 45 min; Refuge de Lure – Pas de la Graille: 2 hrs; total time: 3¾ hrs.

Ascent: About 420m.

Highest point: Signal de Lure, 1826m.

Grade: Well-marked paths and minor roads. Sure-footedness is advisable on the ridge walk.

Alternative: It is possible to descend directly to the road from the summit in 10 min or to miss out on the last loop (at the saddle, about 1700m). The first alternative saves 1¾ hrs, the second 1 hr).

Advice: Even in summer it can be extremely windy on the ridge; bear this in mind in the clothing taken on the walk.

Places of Interest: Sisteron is beautifully situated in a narrow pass of the Durance, the Gate to the Provence. The picturesque old town with its narrow lanes and high houses, the Cathedral of Notre-Dame with its basic Romanesque design, and the Citadel with its splendid views are all attractive to the visitor.

This walk with fine views follows the main ridge of the Montagne de Lure. With the exception of the much-visited main summit, which is »adorned« with a radio mast and offers a fantastic panorama, and some ski lifts in the western part, one can experience much landscape and few people.

From the **car park** take the GR 6 with its red and white waymarks, which leads westwards along the south side of the col to the Signal de Lure. The path rises in stages, mainly not too steep up the southern side of the mountain. First it leads through open scrub and then over barren grazing land. The view now becomes more open. As height is gained the landscape becomes more barren, and the ground is often only covered by thin limestone slabs. After a final uphill section the summit of the **Signal de Lure,**

A wind-blown walker on the ridge to the west of the Signal de Lure.

which is crowned by a radio mast, is reached (1 hr). This is, however, compensated by a splendid panorama, which in clear weather extends to the Alps in the east (Monte Viso), the Pelvoux Massif in the north, the Cevennes in the west, and the Mediterranean in the south. From the summit continue down over a bare slope, still with good views, to a gap where the path touches the road (about 1700m; 15 min). From here there are beautiful views down into the valley of the Jabron. The marked path now climbs gently up a rocky slope on the south side of the ridge to a final rise (1746m; take care on the edge of the ridge, as the ground drops away steeply on the north side!) From here go along for a short section down the ridge, then follow the vague path off to the south to where it meets a forest track, along which, above the **Refuge de Lure**, the road is reached (30 min). Follow the narrow asphalt ribbon to the left on the edge of the forest boundary. The minor road, which as a rule is little-frequented, has three broad loops with only a slight incline on the south side of the Montagne de Lure, and after 45 minutes the previously-mentioned gap is reached (1700m). Now the road is almost level until its vertex at nearly 1750m of height, where a road branches off to the summit (30 min). A further 45 minutes downhill leads back to the **car park**.

42 Ganagobie Plateau

Mediaeval mosaics, beautiful views and rich vegetation

Ganagobie – Allée de Forcalquier – Villevieille – Ganagobie

Location: Manosque, 387m in the Durance Valley.

Starting point: From Manosque drive up the valley along the N 96. About 7km past where the road joins the N 100, take the narrow D 30 on the left, which is winding, has good views, and leads to the monastery (about 650m), 27km from Manosque.

Walking time: Good 1¼ hrs.

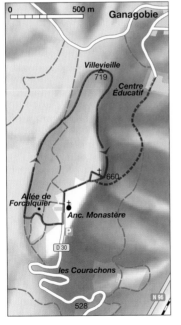

Ascent: Nearly 100m.

Highest point: At Villevieille, 719m.

Grade: Narrow paths in places, but mostly adequately marked, although occasionally on the edge of cliffs. Sure-footedness and a head for heights are necessary.

Alternative: If you wish to avoid the hustle and bustle at the official car park, it is also possible to reach the monastery from the Centre Éducatif de Ganagobie (own access 4km further north from the N 96), via an unmarked footpath (allow an extra hr).

Advice: At present the Monastery of Ganagobie is only open from 15.00 – 17.00 (notice at the beginning of the access road).

Places of Interest: Apart from the Ganagobie mosaics the rocks of Mées also in the valley (north-eastwards), which look like topless earth pyramids, are worth a visit. Manosque is a picturesque old town.

The round trip walk along the plateau with its evergreen chestnut oaks and bushes offers plenty of views, an interesting route and a visit to a unique art monument with its mosaics.

The narrow high path along the wooded plateau of Ganagobie.

From the **car park,** go along a dusty little road in a northerly direction (signpost) for 5 minutes to the monastery (about 660m). Here follow a path with faint red waymarks along a rubble wall, through a forest to the west. At the next junction, go straight on and follow the **Allée de Forcalquier** (fine views) to the western edge of the plateau (10 min). Here take the marked circuit on the right, which runs along the edge of the plateau to the north (take care, vertical cliffs!). After about 15 minutes go to the right above a semi-circle of stones and make a short loop to the right in order to follow a larger transverse path slightly upwards towards the left. This leads again to the edge of the plateau with impressive views into the depths. The path then forks off again to the right and then to the left along a wider path, which is shortly after followed by another path on the left (watch out for the rather unclear markings). Now continue again along the edge of the plateau towards the northernmost point (719m), where the ruins of **Villevieille**, a village destroyed in the middle ages, are found (15 min). Go past the wall which separated the village from the plateau, going around the place in a loop to the right. Then the east edge of the plateau is reached on the left via cliffs. Here there are beautiful views of the Pre-Alps on the other side of the Durance. The marked path now mainly follows the steep drop of the plateau with good views. Continued care is needed. Go past a cross to reach the **monastery** (30 min). The simple Romanesque church contains the remains of wonderfully-coloured floor mosaics from the 12th century. From here it is only 5 minutes back to the **car park**.

43 Gorges de Trévans

A walk of mountainous character in a peaceful but rugged gorge.

Trévans – Valbonnette – Château de Trévans – Trévans

Location: Riez, 528m in the Colostre Valley.
Starting point: From Riez go down along the D 953 in the Asse Valley with good views and then upstream along the D 907 to Estoublon. There take the narrow D 667 rightwards along an isolated stretch to the Gorges de Trévans. After about 5.5km, park at the marked parking area on the right of the road, (600m), 26km from Riez.
Walking time: Car park – Valbonnette: 1½ hrs; Valbonnette – Château de Trévans: nearly 1¾ hrs; Château de Trévans – car park: 50 min; total time: 4 hrs.
Ascent: About 500m.
Highest point: P. 976m.
Grade: Well-marked, but mainly narrow mountain paths, which are exposed in

places and therefore require sure-footedness and a head for heights.
Alternative: The most difficult sections can be avoided, if about 20 min past Valbonnette the path with yellow waymarks is taken, which leads steeply into the valley of the Estoublaisse and 20 min from the car park meets up with the red-marked path (altogether 3 hrs).
Advice: On account of the terrain this walk should be avoided in the case of bad weather.
Places of Interest: A trip to Digne, 22km from Estoublon, is recommended. The main road, lined by plane trees, a small museum for the region and the large Romanesque church are the main attractions.

This walk in the hilly provencale Pre-Alps offers, in contrast to Verdon, more peace and quiet, and surprises one, nevertheless, with its wildness and through its rich vegetation.

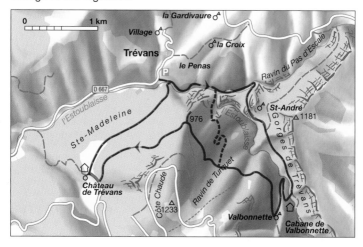

At the beginning of the rugged Gorges de Trévans the cliffs come together.

From the **car park** go along a road in an easterly direction at first along the left side of the river, which is crossed via a bridge, after 5 minutes. Here all the various walks are pictured on a notice board. Follow the path with red markings along the river (sign: »Valbonnette) and so reach the beginning of the **Gorges de Trévans**. The walls come closer together and a section is hewn out of the cliffs. Shortly afterwards a yellow-marked path goes off to the right, which goes up the valley of the Estoublaisse (see alternative). However, go over the stream, walk through a beautiful forest and cross over a tributary stream via a wooden bridge. Up to this point the path mainly runs along the bottom of this impressive, gloomy gorge. Here begins the first steep but short ascent on a rock spur, in order to go around a narrowing. From the rise (30 min) there is a fine view over the rugged landscape. The path leads back down to the Ravin du Pas d'Escale and along the bottom via a dried out ditch. After this there is a wooden bridge over a torrent, which is not always serviceable (then it is necessary to go through the water). The path then leads via a long drawn-out uphill section through a cool forest and after crossing an inconspicuous col turns back into the Trévans Gorge. The well-marked path leads along a rock wall above the gorge: good views but somewhat exposed. After a further 30 minutes a yellow-marked path from the left runs into it (about 800m). Keep going straight on along the stony path with red waymarks, high above the gorge. After this section the path drops down more steeply to the Estoublaisse (ignore a turning off on the left), and cross the river via a wooden bridge (740m). Shortly after the **Cabane de Valbonnette** is reached (750m; 25 min), a base for the forestry administration.

From here follow the red waymarks in a northwesterly direction. In a good 10 minutes the shady forest path leads to a junction at a ruin (825m) where the green markings are followed to the right. Along the easy path the ruins of the village of **Valbonnette** surrounded by some cedars, are passed. After 30 minutes the fork of the yellow-marked variation is reached, which leads rightwards without any problems directly down to the car park (see above). Our route now ascends above the gorge in an interesting garrigue landscape with beech trees and offers fine views downwards. At Point 976m, the highest point of the walk (25 min), there is a yellow-marked path on the left, which leads to the Côte Chaude. However, go straight on along the green-marked path (sign: »Gîte de Trévans«). On the right a short detour to a worthwhile viewpoint over the gorge is possible. Afterwards follows the most difficult section, which should only be undertaken by the sure-footed who have a head for heights. The narrow path leads along a rock band on the edge of the drop into the gorge and offers vertiginous views into the depths. When this section has been overcome the path becomes wider and leads through the wood. Ignoring all turnings off, go downhill as far as a forestry road, which is followed to the right to the nearby **Château** (also **Gîte**) **de Trévans**

The rocky alternative path leads down to the wooded base of the valley.

(about 820m; about 35 min), where there is a forestry administration station. Shortly before this take the red-marked path on the right. It first leads along the level through a small oak wood and then goes down in a number of bends into the valley of the Estoublaisse to the walks notice board mentioned above. Cross over the river (left) and continue downstream to the **car park** (50 min).

44 The Mountains and Forest of Montdenier

An enjoyable high walk with good views and much forest

Car park – Col de Bar Basse – Côte Chaude – Marachare – Car park

Location: Riez, 528m in the Colostre Valley.
Starting point: From Riez drive along the D 953 to Puimoisson. Shortly after the village take the narrower D 108 to St-Jurs, at the beginning of which you take the narrow forestry road on the left to the pass of the same name (sign post). Go through a beautiful forest to a car park with good views at the end of the asphalt (about 1200m), 20km from Riez.
Walking time: Car park – Col de Bar Basse – Côte Chaude: 1¾ hrs; Côte Chaude – Marachare – Car park: 1¼ hrs; total time: 3 hrs.
Ascent: About 330m.
Highest point: About 1270m at Marachare.
Grade: Good tracks without difficulty, which are hardly marked, but which, with a little care, present no navigation problems.
Places of Interest: The Plateau of Valensole offers a magnificent sight in July when the largest lavender fields of the Haute-Provence are covered in their purple splendour.

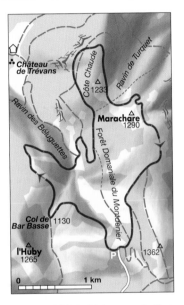

The walk goes through a beautiful forest area which is high up and offers impressive views of the mountains of the Haute-Provence.

From the **car park** first of all enjoy the fine view of the Plateau of Valensole and the Valley of the Asse. Then go down along the approach road for a few metres and in a sharp left-hand bend take the first, closed off forestry track to the right. In an open pine and scrub wood the path goes gently but somewhat rockily downhill to the **Col de Bar Basse** (1130m; 20 min), where the track makes a sharp bend to the right. After a sharp bend the wood becomes thinner and the slope steeper but the view to the north better. After 40 minutes the lowest point in the valley of the Ravin des Béluguettes (about 960m) is reached, where one turns off right. Now continue slightly uphill and soon after take another right. The gravelled track leads up along a moderate incline through open forest and as the height increases the view improves of the Montagne de Lure and the Pre-Alps of Digne. After 45 minutes the

The high route on the Côte Chaude offers a magnificent view into the distance.

northern tip of the **Côte Chaude** ridge is reached, from where a protruding viewpoint provides a broad view of the Pre-Alps in the north. Go around the Côte Chaude along the forestry track in a 180° bend and ignore all turnings off. On the east side of the ridge, which in the heat is not undeserving of its name, go very slightly downhill through low bushes to a sort of saddle. This section is high above the Gorges de Trévans (see Walk 43) and allows impressive views down into the rugged gorge. After a left-hand bend the now rather overgrown track leads gently upwards once again in the shade of the forest and at the rounded top of **Marachare** reaches its highest point (about 1270m). The track continues almost on the flat and there are extensive views of the mountains of the Haute-Provence in the south (Ridge of Montdenier, Chiran, Mourre de Chanier). At a fork (1 hr) go right over the ridge and slightly downhill through the forest to the gravelled forestry track of Col de St-Jurs. Go right again there to soon reach the **car park** (15 min).

45 Cadière de Brandis

Rock throne above Castellane

Col des Lèques – Cadières de Brandis – Col des Lèques

Location: Castellane, 724m in the Verdon Valley.

Starting point: From Castellane drive along the wide N 85 with good views to the Col des Lèques (1146m), 10km from Castellane, where the car can be parked on the side of the road.

Walking time: Col des Lèques – Cadières: nearly 1½ hrs; Cadières – Crête de Colle Bernaiche: 50 min; Colle Bernaiche – Col des Lèques: 1¼ hrs; total time: 3½ hrs.

Ascent: About 450m.

Highest point: About 1600m on the Tête de la Barre de Sapée.

Grade: Mainly forest tracks and paths with satisfactory markings, but due to the craggy terrain, sure-footedness, a head for heights and a sense of direction are absolutely necessary.

Alternative: The ascent to the television mast on the Crête de Colle Bernaiche with its very fine panorama is completely without problems (2¼ hrs there and back).

Advice: In bad weather the walk should not be attempted (navigation problems and slippery rocks below the ridge on the ascent).

Places of Interest: In Castellane the old town with the Church of St-Victor is inviting.

A peaceful, mountain-walk near the Verdon Gorge in a karst landscape with much forest in the lower section and two massive rock monoliths as a crowning finish in the upper section.

At the **height of the pass** take the gravelled forestry track, which leads to the south past a hotel. It is almost level, with yellow waymarkings and offers interesting views into the wooded north flank of the Tête de Barre de la Sapée with its crags. After 10 minutes at a fork (1155m) take the right hand narrower yellow-marked path through a pine forest. About 10 minutes later (P. 1210m) take the marked track on the left, which leads steeply uphill through a gorge in a southerly direction. The track now becomes wider, but is soon left for a path on the left with yellow markings (about 1300m; 20 min). Go steadily upwards through the beech wood of Chalonnet. At the foot of the Barre de la Sapée the track disappears and it is necessary to pay careful

The wooded north side with the summit mass of the Cadière de Brandis.

attention to the markings on the ground. The rugged rock landscape with runnels and sink holes in the limestone, is very impressive. The path is lined with boulders, some of which must be scrambled across. Continue steadily uphill, and shortly after a hollow a natural rock arch is reached (about 1440m) as well as some runnels and sink holes (Take care!) Go over some rocks once again to reach a grass slope on the plateau. The path now improves and shortly after a fork is reached (about 1500m; 45 min). Take the newer yellow markings to the left (the right leads to the **Cadières de Brandis**) and ascend to the highest point of the walk (about 1600m) directly below the south side of the Barre de la Sapée. The path winds its way along here, and after a plateau with large pines there are splendid views of the Verdon and the rock monolith of Cadières. Now cross the ridge and go downhill in an easterly direction via bends. A turning off to the right is ignored and the last section leads almost on the flat to a radio mast on the Crête de Colle Bernaiche (about 1430m; 50 min). Here continue along a forestry track with good views. After a few minutes it is possible at a saddle to continue along the ridge to the summit of the Chalon (1404m; about 20 min there and back, good views). The forestry track now crosses the ridge in a left-hand bend to the north. Shortly after take the marked footpath to the right, which leads down more steeply through a fine coniferous forest to the valley. On reaching the forestry road the steepness decreases noticeably. Ignoring any turnings off, follow the shady forestry track onwards to the fork at a height of 1155m, where the approach path forked off. Return to the starting point on this path (right; 1¼ hrs).

46 Basses Gorges du Verdon

In the little-known but impressive second gorge of the Verdon

Quinson – Basses Gorges du Verdon – St-Maximin – Quinson

Location: Riez, 528m, in the Colostre Valley.
Starting point: From Riez drive along the wide D 11 to Quinson, crossing over the Verdon shortly after the town. Stop immediately after the bridge (364m) on the left by a boat hire place, where adequate parking is available, 21km from Riez.
Walking time: Verdon bridge – Iron stairs: 45 min; Iron stairs – St-Maximin: nearly 1 hr; St-Maximin – P. 549m: 50 min; P. 549m – Verdon bridge: 45 min; total time: 3¼ hrs.
Ascent: Just 200m.
Highest point: P. 549m on the GR 99.
Grade: Generally satisfactory, well-marked paths, which in the gorge are often narrow and a little exposed in places. Handrails and

other safety installations are frequently in a poor state. Sure-footedness and a head for heights are necessary.
Alternative: Anyone without a head for heights should turn back at the iron stairs (about 1½ hrs there and back). This still affords a very fine impression of the gorge.
Advice: Take a torch for the tunnel.
Places of Interest: In Riez four Roman columns are witnesses to a former temple from the earlier settlement. The biggest attraction is the baptistery from the Merovingian period, one of the few remaining building monuments in France from this period.

Although the rock walls do not reach the proportions of those found in the famous main gorge, the walk is, nevertheless, very impressive. The path offers beautiful views in the gorge with a quiet river flowing between the cliffs; the visitor frequency is generally low.

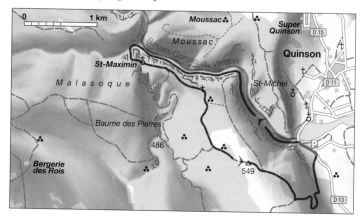

The Verdon bridge and the artificial lake at the beginning of the lower gorge.

From the car park go to the **Verdon bridge** and from there a few paces along the D 13 to the south. Then take the path with yellow waymarks on the right (sign »St-Maximin par Gorges«), which first of all overcomes a rock barrier and then goes along a former water channel, which leads down to the bottom of the **Verdon Gorge**. The Verdon is reached over a new wooden bridge and is followed for a short time. The path then goes up again to the water channel; up to this point there are particularly fine views into the gorge. The path now runs parallel to the abandoned water channel for a longer section, sometimes on its support walls, whereby shade-supplying trees often obstruct the view into the gorge. Handrails and other safety equipment are often in very poor condition and only provide psychological support. Indeed they are often missing altogether. Ignore a turning off to the left to the Plateau Malasoque. The path then leads over some cliffs back to the gorge again, which it follows for a section, partly on a path hewn out of the gorge walls and partly on a wooden platform, until the most worrying section, with the iron stairs is reached (45 min). Having ascended the few metres here, continue along the former water channel. While walking along or next to the support walls there are further beautiful views into the rugged gorge with the sluggishly flowing Verdon. After about 25 minutes a small house is reached at a tunnel, where the water channel ends. Go along the left side of the house and then down an iron ladder into the canal in order to go through the tunnel (a torch is useful here). About 25 metres beyond the tunnel go up another iron ladder on the left-hand side of the canal wall, to turn off left into the valley of the torrent of St-Maximin (370m). The base of the valley, which is followed first in a westerly, then in a southerly direction is covered in box trees. At a junction go up to the left (eastwards) along a rocky, yellow-marked path which winds noticeably uphill in bends, and after 30 minutes the old pilgrimage chapel of **St-Maximin** (467m) is reached. Go in an easterly

direction along the old pilgrim track high above the Verdon gorge, past the square pillar of what was a Calvary and 10 minutes later meet the red and white marked GR 99, which is followed to the left (always following the signs for »Quinson par plateau«). Continue gently uphill through a shady chestnut oak wood. At the height of an old wayside shrine the path takes a right-hand bend, and other turnings off after this are avoided. A couple of ruins are passed on the left (15 min), walk under electric power lines, following the markings on the next turn to the left and reach P. 549m (the highest point of the walk) on the high plateau after hardly any perceptible ascent, (25 min). Juniper bushes and trees dominate the garrigue landscape at this point. Stay for a while on the plateau, taking the next turning right between two

The path through the gorge hewn out of the rocks.

rubble walls, and the next but one turning to the left past the remains of two springs. Now the waymarkings lead back to the left again, and after about 15 minutes there is a splendid view from the edge of the plateau of the lower reaches of the Verdon and its gorges. In spring many lilac-coloured irises flower here. Now the very rocky track of the GR 99 leads down steeply in bends to the D 13, which is then followed to the left back to the starting point (30 min).

The peaceful river and the rugged rock walls in the Basses Gorges du Verdon.

124

47 Lac de Ste-Croix and the lower Verdon

To the artificial lakes of the Verdon and witnesses of the past

Lac de Ste-Croix – Baudinard-sur-Verdon – Valmogne – Rocher aux Trois-Blasons – Pont Sylvestre – Auchier – Lac de Ste-Croix

Location: Riez, 528m in the Colostre Valley.
Starting point: Leave Riez on the D 11 and turn left after 6km onto the D 111. After 16km, cross the Verdon over a bridge at the end of the Lake of Ste-Croix (504m) and park immediately afterwards at one of the car parks there.
Walking time: Lac de Ste-Croix – Baudinard: 1¼ hrs; Baudinard – l'Arbitelle: 1 hr; l'Arbitelle – Pont Sylvestre: 1¼ hrs; Pont – Lac de Ste-Croix: 1½ hrs; total time: 5 hrs.
Ascent: About 350m.

Highest point: 712m at the Chapel of N.-D.-de-la-Garde.
Grade: Satisfactory tracks and minor roads (some tarmac), which are not always marked, and therefore require some ability in navigating; long walk without noteworthy difficulties, but not to be recommended in the heat.
Places of Interest: The varied landscape of Haut-Var to the south, with nice, old towns like Aups, Salernes, Villecroze etc.

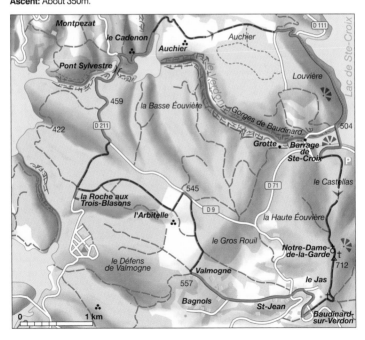

The Verdon Bridge at the dam of Baudinard and the Lac de Ste-Croix.

The walk offers far-reaching views of the lakes and gorges of the lower Verdon and the mountains of the High Provence; on the side of the path cultural jewels await the walker in an area with a charming landscape.

From the **car park** with its beautiful views of the lake and the Gorges de Baudinard, follow the D 71 for a few minutes slightly uphill towards the west (sign: »Baudinard«). At a bend where the road from the lake joins it (526m) goes off to the left along a defile with yellow waymarks. After a steep section it continues left along a little terrace through a thicket of evergreen oaks. Watch out for the markings on this overgrown section. After a sweep to the east, the steepness relents and from a rounded hilltop there is a splendid view of the Lac de Ste-Croix with the mountain chain of Montdenier in the background. Now turn back to the south again and continue to go up along the line of the ridge. Keep to the right at the next two forks, go left at the third one and finally reach the Chapel of Notre-Dame-de-la-Garde (also de Baudinard) via a forestry track with yellow waymarks (712m; 50min). This gives a wonderful view over Lac de Ste-Croix and the mountains of the Haute-Provence. Continue the route towards the south along a slightly downward track, passing an oratorium and a Calvary, keeping to the right at a fork. Where it meets the GR 99 follow the red and white markings to the right (west) and so arrive at **Baudinard** (25 min), a small village with old houses, where the GR is left. Keep as far to the right as possible, thereby reaching the

Fine view of Baudinard-sur-Verdon on the side of the hill.

D 71 (also right) along which one continues to the northwest. At an over-grown cross (613m) turn off left from the D 71 and take the left of two roads (Sign: »5t, 40km/hr«). Go through a farm, keeping to the right (not downhill to the left) and follow the almost-level tarmac road. Ignore a track on the right and a minor road on the left. Go past a transformer building and down a slight hill to the **Valmogne** Abbey, where the asphalt ends (557m; 30 min). If you ask the friendly owner, you will certainly be able to visit the beautiful Romanesque building with an early Christian baptistery (5th cent). After the abbey turn right into a defile with a natural surface which leads through a lavender field until a track crossing it is met. Take this, now with yellow waymarks again, towards the west and so reach the D 9. Follow this for about 150 metres to the left (545m) and then go left again along the ap-proach road to the farm of **l'Arbitelle**, where the remains of an old mill are to be found (30 min). Go past the farmyard to the west along the edge of a field, until a forestry road is met at the edge of a forest. Go along this to the northeast into the forest and turn off after a few metres along the yellow-mar-ked track. On the other side of the Verdon the little village of Montpezat can be seen in a dominating position high above the valley. At a large clearing follow the hardly-visible, yellow-marked path over flat stone slabs. After a forestry administration barrier it becomes a road and leads with somewhat intermittent markings to a crossing. Here go left along a tarmac road. Shortly afterwards, just past a sharp bend, take a track on the left, which quickly becomes narrower and leads between evergreen oaks to the **Rocher aux Trois-Blasons** (35 min), where three artistic coats of arms from 1743 are cut in relief in the rock. Go back along the same track to the tarmac road, then go right slightly uphill to the end of the tarmac at the above-mentioned crossing and now go straight on along the gravelled track. Without taking any notice of a turning off, after a short uphill section the D 211 is reached, which leads rapidly downhill to the **Pont Sylvestre**, the lowest point of the walk (about 525m; 40 min) where there are fine views of a small lake to the right and the Basses Gorges du Verdon to the left. After the bridge go uphill for a few minutes along the tarmac road and then take the first gravelled track on the right. Go straight on at the next crossing, then left, down to a small lake and then along its bank. The track now goes up to a plateau – keep right at a fork – and goes close to the ruins of **Auchier** (35 min). Bearing right again at the next fork, there is soon a wonderful view of Lac de Ste-Croix. At the following two crossings go straight on and right respectively down to the D 111, which leads to the right back to the **car park** at the Verdon Bridge (nearly 1 hr).

The broad surface of the Lac de Ste-Croix near the dam.

48 In the Forêt de la Repentance

Excursion into the realm of pines and lavender

Le Moulin – Pylône – St-Clair – le Moulin

Location: Moustiers-Ste-Marie, 631 m.
Starting point: From Moustiers first drive along the D 952, then the D 957 to the south and after 4 km park at the »le Moulin« campsite (490 m) on the side of the road.
Walking time: Car park – Radio mast: 1½ hrs; Radio mast – D 957: nearly 1¼ hrs; D 957 – Car park: 35 min; total time: 3¼ hrs.
Ascent: About 280 m.
Highest point: About 770 m at the radio mast (Pylône).
Grade: Satisfactory tracks and minor roads, which are not very demanding; at times, however, a sense of direction is necessary as not all of the stretch is marked or signposted.
Places of Interest: Moustiers is famous for its splendid faience, which can be seen in a small museum, and for the picturesque situation of the old town with narrow little lanes built on cliffs on both sides of a gorge. The old church with its Romanesque tower and its gothic choir, and the chapel of Notre-Dame-de-Beauvoir above the town, and with a splendid view, are also worth a visit.

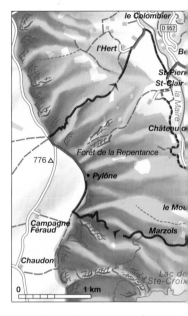

This walk stands out through its contrast-rich landscape: green forests, purple lavender fields, the blue lake of Ste-Croix and the light-coloured mountain slopes above Moustiers.

From the **car park,** cross over the Maire on the approach road to the campsite. Immediately after the bridge turn left along the road with yellow waymarks and at the next crossroads turn right into the plane tree avenue. Shortly after this there is a barrier. After a left-hand bend, go to the right past an estate, cross a field and finally reach the forest. After crossing under high-tension cables, take the first forest track on the right, which leads slowly up through a pine wood, more or less parallel to the electricity cables. Ignore any smaller paths that turn off; repeatedly there are fine views of Moustiers. After about 35 minutes a forestry administration barrier and a sign prohibiting driving are reached: immediately turn right here onto a track. Stay on this to

On the ascent through the Forêt de la Repentance.

the left and go up via zigzags in an open forest to the left of the electricity cables. After a ruin on the left, cross under the cables once again. Shortly after this there are views of the lake. In the course of the continued zigzag ascent, there are again fine views of Moustiers from above a deep ditch. At the end of the ascent after another forestry barrier the road meets the red and white waymarkings of the GR 4 at Campagne Féraud (766m; 45 min), and this is followed to the right. This continues almost on the flat on the edge of a plateau and 10 minutes later passes a **radio mast** (about 770m). Now the road is tarred, and the walk continues comfortably to the right of huge lavender fields, which are full of purple flowers in July, occasionally interrupted by fields of cereal. Shortly after the junction with the local road in the direction of Moustiers (straight on here; 15 min) the waymarked GR forks off to the right at the signpost »Forêt Domaniale du Montdenier« into the forest and is followed fairly steeply, and with numerous bends, down the hill. There are again fine views of Moustiers along this section. Minor turnings off are ignored and a gravelled track is reached. Keep following the GR waymarks and turn right at the next crossroads (45 min) in a southeasterly direction. At the following larger fork take the marked minor road on the left, which then crosses the Maire and meets the D 952 (10 min). This is followed to the right until after about 500 metres at the left fork of the D 952 and GR 4 (527m), the D 957 is followed straight on. After about 1.5km slightly downhill, and after passing a small lake, the starting point is reached again (35 min).

49 Moustiers-Ste-Marie and the Ravin du Riou

A walk which avoids the crowds of tourists in the picturesque Moustiers

Moustiers-Ste-Marie – Ravin du Riou and back

Location: Moustiers-Ste-Marie, 631m.
Starting point: Spacious car park in the town at the Post Office (signposted).
Walking time: Moustiers-Ste-Marie – Ravin du Riou: good 1½ hrs; Return via the same route: good 1¼ hrs; total time: a little under 3 hrs.

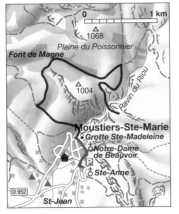

Ascent: About 420m.
Highest point: About 960m.
Grade: Mainly satisfactorily marked tracks, which present no particular difficulties, but rather exhausting if it is hot.
Advice: Do not try to go back along the Ravin du Riou to Moustiers. This walk through difficult terrain is only possible for experienced climbers with suitable equipment.
Places of Interest: See previous walk.

From the idyllic town of Moustiers the path leads below steep crags and through the typical landscape of the Haute-Provence with fine views to a shady picnic spot in the green valley of the Ravin du Riou.

From the **car park,** go past the post office and the Faience Museum in the direction of the town centre. Shortly before the main road go right, up the Rue de la Bourgade, which is lined by decorative Faience shops on the right and the gorge of the Ravin de Notre-Dame on the left. Cross over the torrent via an old bridge noticing a chapel which nestles like an eagle's nest on the top of the steep, towering crags. The Place J.-B. Pommey, with beautiful old houses, is reached and then go upwards to the right along the Rue de la Clappe (sign: »Cascade«). Ignore the turning off to a cave on the right. The tarmac road now has yellow waymarks and leads along almost on the level.

The evening sun on the cliffs of Moustiers-Ste-Marie.

Moustiers, uniquely-situated at the foot of steep cliffs.

There are fine views of Moustiers with its splendid position below steep crags. Shortly after the **Ravin du Riou** is crossed via a mediaeval bridge (waterfall on the right). A few minutes later turn off to the right onto a rocky track with yellow waymarks (direction: »Vincel«) which leads up through olive trees and later pines and young cedars (steep in places). At the next cross-roads (30 min) again follow the yellow waymarks to the right (sign: »Vincel«). Along the continuation of the walk there are beautiful views of the lavender-covered plateau of Puimoisson and the blue-green lake of Ste-Croix. The track now winds up between the edge of the forest and the typical garrigue vegetation. On the northwest horizon the Lure and Luberon mountains appear along with Mont Ventoux. In a high pine forest the path becomes

shadier and more level; it leads through a wooded gorge between two mountaintops. At a fork with a cairn (about 960m) follow the track with yellow waymarks to the left through craggy terrain until it meets a forestry track (50 min), although is followed downhill to the right (yellow waymarks). Stay on this track, where, somewhat later the yellow markings go off to the left. The path winds down, partly in the forest, into the green basin of the Ravin du Riou (about 860m; 15 min). This is lined by shady willows, and its gentle impression provides a pleasant contrast to the otherwise harsher landscape of garrigue vegetation and bare rock faces.

The walk returns via the same route (good 1¼ hrs).

50 The Great Verdon Gorge

The most splendid gorge in Europe

Chalet de la Maline – Brèche d'Imbert – Couloir Samson – Point Sublime

Location: Moustiers-Ste-Marie, 631m.
Starting point: From Moustiers drive along the wide panoramic D 952 up the Verdon Valley towards la Palud. There take the D 23 rightwards (fine views) to the Chalet de la Maline (893m) a refuge hut belonging to the CAF, 28km from Moustiers.
End of Walk: Auberge du Point Sublime (783m) on the D 952. Return journey to Chalet de la Maline by taxi.
Walking time: La Maline – Brèche d'Imbert: nearly 2½ hrs; Brèche d'Imbert – 2nd Tunnel: 2¾ hrs; 2nd Tunnel – Point Sublime: 50 min; total time: 6 hrs.
Ascent/Descent: About 470m of descent and 350m of ascent.
Lowest point: 558m in gorge.
Grade: Adequate, well-marked paths, but

The entrance to the long tunnel.

The harmless Aesculapius snake – here in the first tunnel – grows up to two metres in length.

not always very wide. Sure-footedness and a head for heights are required, particularly on the steep metal steps.
Alternative: From P. 633m there is a worthwhile spur path, which leads off to Mescla, the junction of the Verdon and the Artuby, at which the latter forms a narrower gorge; about 30 minutes, there and back.
Advice: A torch is indispensable for the 700m-long tunnel at the end. In summer, especially at weekends, there are a lot of people in the gorge. Only undertake the walk in good weather, as due to the narrowness of the gorge, thunderstorms can only be noticed late on and they can be pretty severe.
Places of Interest: The walk should be completed by a drive around the gorge on the wide, panoramic road (D 952, D 23 to the north, D 71 to the south) on both sides of the river, which has numerous vantage points from which unforgettable views into the depths of the mighty gorge can be obtained.

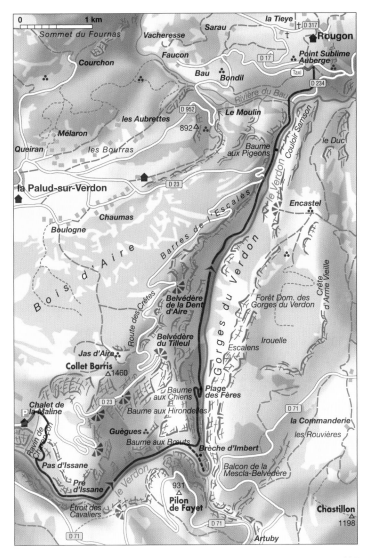

la Tieye

Sarau

Rougon

Sommet du Fournas

Vacheresse

Courchon

Faucon

Point Sublime
Auberge

D 17

Bau

Bondil

Taxi

D 234

Rivière du Bau

les Aubrettes

D 952

Le Moulin

Mélaron

892△

Queiran

les Bourras

Baume
aux Pigeons

le Duc

Coulior Sanson

la Palud-sur-Verdon

D 23

le Verdon

Encastel

Chaumas

Boulogne

Barres de l'Escalès

Gorges du Verdon

Bois d'Aire

Forêt Dom. des
Gorges du Verdon

Crête
d'Arme Vieille

Belvédère
de la Dent
d'Aire

Route des Crêtes

Belvédère
du Tilleul

Escalens

Irouelle

Jas d'Aire

Collet Barris
△1460

Chalet de
la Maline

D 23

Baume
aux Chiens

Plage
des Fères

D 71

Baume aux Hirondelles

Ravin de Mainmorte

la Commanderie
les Rouvières

Guègues

Baume aux Bouts

Pas d'Issane

Pré
d'Issane

le Verdon

Brèche d'Imbert

Balcon de la
Mescla-Belvédère

Etroit des
Cavaliers

931
△
Pilon
de Fayet

D 71

Chastillon
1198

D 71

Artuby

The Grand Canyon du Verdon can be described as the smaller brother of the North-American Grand Canyon. The accessible section along the Sentier Martel offers an incomparable experience in this grandiose natural wonder.

From the CAF **Chalet de la Maline** (893m) take the red and white waymarked GR 4, which first leads slighty downhill through the gorge of the Ravin de Charençon. After this it goes via the Pas d'Issane steeply down into the gorge with bends and steps. After 50 minutes, keep left at a junction (628m; a bridge over the river on the right) and after a few bends reach a point about 10 metres above the river. Now follow the river upstream on its right bank; high crags line both sides of the gorge. On the opposite side of the river the Auberge des Cavaliers appears like an eagle's nest. Now it is possible on the pleasant track to enjoy the beauties of the gorge to the full. The valley widens, the Pré d'Issane, a small meadow, is passed and the lowest point is reached (558m; about 30 min). After this the Guègues scree slope has to be overcome. There is a short uphill and steep downhill section with scree and crags, partly via metal ladders, so that some care is required. Shortly after this, the Baume aux Bœufs is reached (30 min) – a sort of cave in which pre-historic cattle bones were found. The path goes up now to reach a fork in 10 minutes (633m). Stay to the left on the red and white marked Sentier Martel (right: see alternative) which winds steeply up over rock steps to a gap in the rocks: **Brèche d'Imbert** (710m; about 25 min). This is named after the engineer who opened up this passage for the walker. From here there is a fascinating view of the Verdon rushing through the gorge over 100 metres below. This height difference is overcome by means of a steep, ladder-like, but solid metal staircase with over 200 steps; despite all caution this is a problematic section for the timid. After a short section along the river the walk continues uphill again below the Baume aux Hirondelles to then to descend again more steeply in a double loop at the Baume aux Chiens to the river at the Plages des Fères (about 570m; 50 min). It again goes up and down, while on the opposite bank the 500 metre-high rock wall of Escalès, an Eldorado for rock-climbers, towers above. Now the delightful section of the gorge is reached where it widens. The path continues with very little change in height about 30 metres above the river, mainly through a shady wood. After a first – no longer passable – tunnel and a few metal steps there is a beautiful backward view to the twin cliffs of Trescaïre. Now go through an approximately 100 metre-long tunnel, which leads to the entrance to the **Couloir Samson**, a narrow rock passage through the cliffs. This is avoided by an almost 700 metre-long, pitch-dark tunnel, where a torch is indispensable and which is quite slippery on account of the dripping water. The descent from a tunnel window via an iron ladder to the Baume aux Pigeons cave was closed the last time. At the end of the tunnel go down over some steps to the river below (610m; nearly 2 hrs) and take a look into the rugged couloir. Then cross a tributary and go up steeply over steps to a car

Dizzying view down into the Gorges du Verdon.

park (sometimes taxis). At its left-hand end take the red and white marked path (GR 4), which ascends steeply to the D 952, which is followed to the left for about 150 metres to the **Auberge du Point Sublime** (783m, 50 min). From here return by taxi to the starting point of la Maline.

The towns of Arles, Nîmes and Avignon

Nobody should visit the Provence without planning a visit to the three towns, which are among the most beautiful towns in France, combining ancient, mediaeval and modern at close quarters.

Arles

Arles is distinguished by its splendid ancient and mediaeval buildings, as well as through its museums and its atmosphere.

From the car park at the post office at the edge of the old town go along the plane-tree lined *Boulevard des Lices* and cross diagonally leftwards through the beautiful park of Jardin d'Été to the **Ancient Theatre** (1st cent BC) from which only a part of the stage wall and the auditorium remain standing. From the north side one comes to the right through the *Rue de la Calade* to the **Amphitheatre** (1st cent AD; for 25,000 spectators). Now go west along the *Rue des Arènes* to the *Place du Forum* and further right along the *Rue de l'Hôtel de Ville*, at the end of which are found the remains of the Thermal baths from the one-time **Imperial Palace** and the **Museum Réattu** (16th – 20th century paintings). Now go along the main road back to the north edge of the *Place de la République*, to then turn off to the right into *Rue Balze*. There is found the **Museum of Christian Art** (early Christian sarcophagus) and the **Cryptoportico**, an underground columned hall which served as a granary. At the end of Rue Balze turn left and left again (via Rue Mistral) into the *Rue de la République* with the **Museon Arlaten** and so to the *Place de la République*, on the left of which is found the **Museum for Non-Christian Art** (ancient sarcophagi, statues, busts and mosaics) and the **Town Hall** (17th cent, clock tower). On the opposite side is the mediaeval pride of Arles, the Romanesque church of **St-Trophime** (splendid relief-decorated portal), interior with tapestries and paintings, cloi-ster). From the church go in a southerly direction (Rue de l'Hôtel de Ville) along the *Boulevard des Lices* past the excavations of the **Esplanade** to the left into *Rue E. Fassin*. Follow a canal and go straight on along the *Av. des Alyscamps* as far as the cemetery of the same name with the ruin of the Romanesque Church of St-Honorat. From there go back to the starting point.

Nîmes

The spacious, elegant city has well-preserved Roman monuments, museums worth visiting and a beautiful park.

From the *Place de la Libération* (good place to park) follow the *Rue Briconnet* in a south-easterly direction and then go right into the *Rue Bourdaloue* as far as the *Rue de la Cité Foulc*, where diagonally to the left the **Musée des Beaux-Arts** (Roman finds, 15th – 19th century paintings) is to be found. Now go back along the *Rue de la Cité Foulc* to the **Amphitheatre** (2nd century; 24,000 spectators), the most beautiful and best preserved in the Provence. From the arena go along the elegant *Boulevard V. Hugo* to the north-west and then right via the *Rue Perrier* to the Roman temple **Maison Carrée** (1st century BC; Corinthian columns outside, a coffered ceiling and a worthwhile museum). From the temple follow the *Rue Auguste* straight on to the *Square Antonin* and go left there to the *Quai de la Fontaine*, to go into the **Jardin de la Fontaine** opposite the *Av. J. Jaurès* (right). This is a beautiful garden from the 18th century, which was laid out according to baroque principles. Now in a northerly direction past the Diana Temple, go on to the 34 metre high **Magne-Tower** (1st century BC; splendid panorama). From the Tower take the first right, the *Rue S. Mallarmé*, go right again along the *Rue Rouget de Lisle* and then left along the *Rue d'Albénas* to **Castellum** (end of the water supply from the Pont du Gard). Here go right into the *Rue de la Lampèze* and then diagonally left over the *Rue du Fort* to the *Boulevard Gambetta*, which is followed to the east past the house where the poet Daudet was born (no 20) to the *Place Péri* with its Roman town gate **Porte d'Auguste** (15 BC). Now go down the Boulevard Courbet to the right to the Archaeological Museum (gallic-roman discoveries). After the museum go to the right via the *Rue des Greffes* to the mediaeval part of the town. Via the *Grande Rue* and the *Rue du Chapitre* the *Place du Chapitre* is reached with its **Local History Museum** and the **Cathedral**. Continue via the *Place aux Herbes* and the *Rue Madeleine* in a westerly direction as far as the *Rue de l'Aspic*, which is followed to the left. The circuit ends at the Amphitheatre.

Avignon

The mediaeval, completely-walled old town, with its narrow alleys, historical places of interest and museums, has something to offer for everybody.

Enter the old town via the **Porte de l'Oulle** (good place to park) and go left into the *Rue du Rempart-du-Rhône* and follow the mediaeval town wall (14th cent) which encloses the centre of the town. At the end of the street go up right to the Cathedral rock. At half height it is possible to make a detour left to the symbol of Avignon, the mediaeval **Bridge of St-Bénézet**, which is crowned by a chapel. From the original 22 arches only 4 remain, so that the bridge ends in the river. From the papal park on the Rocher des Doms there is a wonderful panorama. On the left a visit to the **Petit Palais** (Collection of paintings by Italian Masters) is worthwhile, the **Cathedral** situated to the south has many baroque characteristics and has the late gothic gravestone of Pope John XXII. After this go on to the biggest mediaeval monument of the city, the sombre, austere **Papal Palace**

(14th cent; chapel frescos, deer room); opposite the **Hôtel des Monnaies** (17th cent). From the Cathedral rock go down to the east via the streets J.Vilar, Peyrollerie and Vice-Légat and left into the *Rue Banasterie*. Go past the splendid house no 13 to the baroque chapel of the Black Penitents (**Pénitents Noirs**). From here go right via the *Rue des 3 Colombes* to *Place Joseph*, and diagonally right along the *Rue Palapharnerie* to the *Place des Carmes* (entrance via the Rue des Infirmières). At the **Church of St-Symphorien** is the cloister of the one-time monastery. Go past the bell tower of the Augustinian monastery, then left along *Rue Carreterie* and straight on along *Rue Carnot* back into the old town to the late gothic **Church of St-Pierre**. Go past the interesting **Hôtel de Rascas** and south along the narrow *Rue des Fourbisseurs* to *Place St-Didier* with the gothic **Church of St-Didier** (fine altarpiece, rich frescos). From the square take the *Rue du Roi René*, which is lined by beautiful old houses, in an easterly direction, and continue along the similar *Rue de la Masse*. Then turn right and right again, first into the *Rue de la Bonneterie*, then into the *Rue des Lices* (later Rue H. Fabre), from which a short detour to the right to the **Musée Lapidaire** (gallic-roman finds) in the Rue de la République is worthwhile. The Rue Fabre continues straight on into the Rue J.Vernet – here is the **Calvet Museum** (works of 16th –20th century French painters). From the museum take the *Rue H.Vernet* on the right, the *Rue Bouquerie* on the left, and the *Rue Viala* on the right to the *Rue de la République*, which one follows to the left to the *Place de l'Horloge* with the **Town Hall** (mediaeval Clock Tower). From the north side of the Square go via the Rue Molière, the Rue Racine, the Rue St-Etienne, the Rue J.Vernet and the Rue Folco-de-Baroncelli back to the Porte de l'Oulle.

Index